Financing
California
Government

Financing
California
Government

Gerhard N. Rostvold   Consulting Economist, Claremont, California

Dickenson Publishing Company, Inc., Belmont, California

To Ellen

The verse on page 62, from Principles of Economic Policy *by Kenneth E. Boulding,* © *1958 by Prentice-Hall, Inc., is reprinted by permission of the publisher.*

L.C. Cat. Card No.: 67–14176
Printed in the United States of America

Editor's Foreword

California law requires every student who attends a California university, college, or junior college to receive instruction in California state and local government before he is admitted to degree status. In view of the compulsory nature of this instruction, it is imperative that the literature on the subject be of a quality that will stimulate and satisfy intellectual curiosity. It is always a matter of despair when the textbooks in a field fail to match the importance that has been assigned to it. When the State of California enacted the California government course requirement, it acknowledged that instruction in this subject was as important as instruction in any of the other social sciences, natural sciences, or the humanities.

Until this California Government Series was inaugurated, there was no single work or set of works that examined the California political system in depth. In the five or six other currently available texts, the subject is compressed into 118 to 298 pages, with the average chapter 21 pages in length. Obviously, it is a difficult task to include in so brief a space all that needs to be said about the various activities and agencies of California state government. Many institutions have endeavored to satisfy the requirement by joining California state and local government to a course on American government, California history, or the U.S. Constitution. It is not unusual in such a situation to find that attention to California government is constricted, put off until the last few weeks of the term, and taught in such a way that little attention is given to local government due to a propensity to emphasize state government in so brief a presentation.

This integrated series of seven books has been prepared because a more expert analysis is possible when diverse specialists write in the field of their authority. Moreover, the series' approach—with over 800 pages of text—makes it possible to expand to three to six chapters what is now dispatched in one or two chapters in one-volume texts. The focus is not on a ponderous description of California's institutions and laws but rather on the dynamic way that these have been adapted to deal with the physical, social, and economic problems that grip the state. Where problems remain unsolved, they are acknowledged and presented in a way that should stimulate imagination and concern. Experiences and practices of governments in other states are introduced when appropriate and useful. In addition, each book gives almost equal space to the state and local levels of government, affording students the unique opportunity to make a systematic comparison of the two levels of government within the same functional setting.

Thomas J. Ashley

Contents

Tables

Preface

A dual theme provides the general framework for this study of California's state-local tax system. The first is grounded on the proposition that the tax system should be tied directly to economic growth measured in terms of increasing income, output, and employment; the second theme relates to the simple fact that an urban-industrial society places greater responsibilities on state and local units of government than did the agricultural society of decades now long past. The processes of urbanization and industrialization inevitably translate themselves into increased public costs that must be financed if orderly economic growth and community life are to be realized.

One of the primary objectives of this study is to establish that there is a direct relationship between California's rapid population and economic growth and the functions traditionally performed by state and local units of government. The brunt of the argument rests on the proposition that California has unlimited economic growth potential; the validity of this argument rests on the further proposition that an adequate state-local revenue system is an absolute prerequisite to the realization of the ultimate economic potential measured in terms of employment, personal income, and gross state product.

Whenever a question in taxation is debated, one should be aware of the philosophical, economic, political, and general social aspects of the points at issue. Each of these dimensions has a proper place in the public policy formula used in solving the problems of taxation in modern society. It is fallacious to assume an absolute position with respect to any one of these variables. All are relevant to the development of a tax system compatible with the values, goals, institutions, and basic underlying philosophy of the society itself.

This volume on the California state-local revenue system is organized along the following lines: Chapter 1 is devoted to a brief factual description and analysis of the population and economic growth forces at work in the California economy since 1940; Chapter 2 explores the main facets of local public finance; Chapter 3 considers the State's fiscal system; Chapter 4 develops a policy framework within which to construct a modern state-local system of taxation; Chapter 5 encompasses an analysis of the manner in which state-local tax burdens are distributed in California; finally, Chapter 6 probes the fiscal future and outlines a proposed program of finance compatible with the urbanization and economic forces that will condition California's development in the decades ahead.

In the preparation of this study, the author received invaluable assistance in the form of materials, discussion, and guidance from many people. Among these, I would like to give explicit recognition to Hale Champion, State Director of Finance; Bert A. Betts, State Treasurer; Richard Nevins, California State Board of Equalization; Nicholas C. Petris, Chairman of the Assembly Revenue and Taxation Committee; Houston Flournoy, State Controller; Philip E. Watson, Assessor, Los Angeles County; and Fred Sharp, Administrative Officer, Pomona, California. I am also deeply in the debt of the academic economists and others who prepared the recent state senate and assembly studies. I have drawn heavily from these. To that great teacher and student of public finance, Elmer D. Fagan, I will always be indebted; he gave me a genuine appreciation of the linkage between the philosophical and the economic aspects of taxation. Miss Mildred Smith, who typed the manuscript from a hand-written first draft, deserves special recognition. It goes without saying that any and all deficiencies of this work are the responsibility of the author.

G.N.R.

The third and last duty of the sovereign or common-wealth is that of erecting and maintaining those public institutions and those public works, which, though they may be in the highest degree advantageous to a *great society,* are, however, of such a nature, that the profit could never repay the expense to any individual or small number of individuals, and which it there-fore cannot be expected that any individual or small number of individuals should erect or maintain. The performance of this duty requires too very different degrees of expense in the different periods of society. —Adam Smith, *The Wealth of Nations.* [Emphasis added.]

The public costs of economic growth and urbanization

> Governments existing by the will of the governed are destined to be confronted with fiscal problems, since free peoples seem to have both a large appetite for governmental services and the means of expressing their instinctive aversion to taxes.
>
> —*Commission on Intergovernmental Relations*

1

As indicated in the Preface, this study has two basic themes. On the one hand it is suggested that California has the economic means for meeting the increasing public costs associated with its transition from an agriculturally-based to an urban-industrial economy. Consistent with this thesis is the recommendation that the state-local tax system be geared to such economic indicators as gross state income and product, personal income, and other appropriate measures of economic power—and tax-paying capacity—in an urban-industrial age.

It is suggested, further, that population and economic growth translate themselves directly into higher absolute and relative public costs that must ultimately be borne by economic units, i.e., households and business enterprises within the private sector. There is no escape from this conclusion as long as the social institutions of private property and private enterprise are dominant characteristics of the American social scene.

In this chapter the relationships between economic and urban growth forces and the state-local system of public finance are explored. These are inextricably bound together. Accordingly, an analysis of the system of taxation must be conducted within the context of the population and economic growth factors which, in turn, create the need for new state-local tax revenues.

California's population growth since 1940

Rapid population growth has been one of the main factors giving impetus and sustained support to California's economic development during the past several decades. From a level of 1.5 million persons in 1900, the state's population approached 7.0 million in 1940, and increased to 10.5 million by 1950. Between 1950 and 1960, population increased by 5.0 million; by the end of 1965, over 19.0 million persons resided in California.

Table 1. California's population
1900–1965
millions

Year	Population	Year	Population
1900	1.5	1940	6.9
1910	2.4	1950	10.6
1920	3.4	1960	15.7
1930	5.7	1965	19.0

Sources: U.S. Census and California State Department of Finance.

Stated another way, in each 24-hour period of the decade of the 1950's, California's population increased an average of 1,400 persons. During 1960, in-migration added 1,000 persons every 24 hours; internal growth sources added another 650 each day, for a total daily population increment of 1,650. These population growth rates are being maintained, and there is reasonable certainty that they will be maintained, if not exceeded, in future decades.

Of great relevance to the matter of state-local finance is the fact that over 85.0 percent of the state's population is concentrated in ten urban centers. The forces of urbanization unquestionably generate an increase in demand for those public goods and services, e.g., police and fire protection, traditionally provided by state and local units of government.

Certain socio-economic characteristics of California's growing population also have a direct bearing upon the present and future fiscal responsibilities of government. In terms of age distribution, the population is relatively young and it will grow younger, as evidenced by increasing enrollment in the education system of the state.

Contrary to general impression, California is not populated disproportionately by retired persons over 65 years of age. In 1960, 9.23 percent of the population of the United States was over 65 years of age; 8.76 percent of California's 1960 population was of retirement age. Many persons of retirement age are living on limited incomes; one of the contemporary issues in California taxation is concerned with the manner in which local property tax burdens impinge upon lower-income households of retirement age.

Table 2. Population growth in selected California counties 1940–1965

	Population Increase
The "Bay Area metropolis"	
Marin	130,000
San Francisco	150,000
San Mateo	412,000
Santa Clara	682,000
Alameda	500,000
Contra Costa	400,000
Solano	110,000
Total	2,384,000
The "Southern California metropolis"	
Los Angeles	4,000,000
Orange	1,000,000
San Diego	1,000,000
Ventura	200,000
Santa Barbara	200,000
Riverside	300,000
San Bernardino	500,000
Total	7,200,000

Sources: U.S. Census and California State Department of Finance.

The citizens of California, it is suggested, manifest one common trait—diversity. Many, if not most of us, are newcomers; we are highly mobile; few of us work or shop in the city or suburb in which we live; we are culturally diverse; we come from many walks of life; we are employed in diverse lines of production; our leisure interests are many and varied; we live in a dynamic and unique urban environment characterized by a low density land-use pattern; the automobile is our main mode of mass transit; our total population is growing younger in terms of age-distribution, yet the retired person is an important segment of each community.

There is, in other words, no original model or prototype of the contemporary Californian. Rather, he is a study in contrast: he is youth and retiree; he is immigrant and native; he is single-family and apartment dweller; he is skilled and educated, unskilled and lacking in educational opportunity; most commute by automobile, few by bus; he is minority and majority; mobile and anchored; promoter and missionary; wealthy and poor. More than anything, he is inextricably a part of a state that is destined to become even more highly urbanized and industrialized with the passage of time.

These diverse characteristics of the California population are, in part, the cause of a lack of social cohesiveness. Many newcomers to California, for example, do not become involved in the life and the issues of the community. This has significant implications relating to the ability of state and local units to develop a system of taxation which will finance at least the current operating costs generated by the growth process.

The sheer growth in population, and the diverse socio-economic characteristics of the citizenry, have an important bearing on the fiscal responsibilities of state and local government. Population growth translates itself into the formation of new household units. Recent estimates by the author suggest that each new household unit in an urban area of California creates a simultaneous demand for at least $15,000 of public capital goods—classrooms, police and fire protection, equipment and facilities, freeways, water and waste disposal systems, etc.

The urban growth process, to put it bluntly, is very costly. Yet few citizens are willing to recognize the cost or the problem aspects of population growth.

The inherent relationship between the private and public sectors of the society finds its most direct means of expression in the economic principle of complementarity. This principle holds that an increase in demand for one type of economic good creates a simultaneous increase in demand for a complementary good. Thus, an increase in the demand for automobiles will result in an increase in demand for tires, gasoline, auto repairs and services.

The principle of complementarity applies interchangeably to many private and public goods. The purchase of a new automobile—a privately produced good, valued in terms of market selling price—creates a simultaneous demand for a public road and freeway system, traffic control service, etc. The private developer, in building a new subdivision, is setting the stage for a simultaneous increase in citizen demand for a host of public goods and services: water and waste disposal systems, police and fire protection, recreation facilities, and an education system.

If orderly community and economic growth conditions are to be realized in our expanding urban areas, citizens and business enterprises must be willing to allocate an appropriate share of their increasing incomes to finance the goods and services demanded from the public sector. We tend to lose sight of the fact that it is the citizen—whether as householder or businessman—who demands a first-class freeway, disposal, education, and protection system. These demands are not created by Madison Avenue-types in Sacramento or in the council chambers of California's municipalities.

California's economic development since 1940

It has been suggested that issues in taxation have philosophical, political, social, and economic dimensions, and that each of these must be an integral part of the framework of analysis. One paramount aspect of the process of taxation is concerned with the effects of taxes on economic productivity and incentives in the private sector. Needless to say, the economic impact of the system of taxation is an exceedingly important matter in a private enterprise-oriented system.

By its nature, a private enterprise system places highest priority on the rights of the individual in the protection of his property, his income, his pursuit of life, liberty and happiness. In a capitalistic system the property rights in economic resources are held by persons in the private sector. These economic resources are the source of the money income which, in turn, commands real goods and services.

It is patently obvious, yet we often tend to ignore the fact, that units of government in a democratic system do not hold property rights in economic resources, and, as a consequence, do not hold primary, or prior, claims to money and real income with which to finance public expenditures. Governmental units must resort to the financial processes of taxation or borrowing for this purpose.

The process of taxation, in particular, represents a direct encroachment upon individual freedom and property rights. The element of compulsion associated with taxation carries with it an inherent conflict between the individual's rights and the social interest. The essence of this conflict is philosophical, and attitudes toward government's role in the society are conditioned accordingly.

The primary barrier to an adequate state-local system of taxation is not economic. It is in large part philosophic. Most people simply hate to pay taxes. The problem is largely one of the individual's attitude toward the governmental processes. As long as this attitude persists, the Galbraithian "social imbalance" between private and public goods, e.g., automobiles and freeways, will typify the California scene.[1]

Attitudes toward taxation based on philosophical underpinnings are one thing; the question of the real economic capacity of a society to bear the costs of government is another. It is this latter dimension of the taxation process which is of concern at this point. The question is posed, "Does California have the economic capability of financing the *socially desirable* level of state-local expenditures required as a result of existing and contemplated urban and industrial growth?" In other words, can California afford to allocate a large enough portion of its money and real income (through taxation and new bond flotations) to command real economic resources in sufficient quantity to produce the public goods and services compatible with orderly growth? We will support the proposition that the state of California does indeed have the economic capability of financing the public costs of growth.

California's economic development during the past several decades has been spectacular. Despite periodic cyclical adjustments in the national economy, California's level of employment, personal income, and value of goods and services produced have grown almost without interruption over the past quarter of a century. With the exception of minor

[1] Galbraith, J.K., *The Affluent Society* (Houghton Mifflin, 1958).

declines in the postwar transition of 1944–1945 and the first postwar recession in 1948–1949, the level of civilian employment in California has grown each year since 1940. The levels of personal income and value of production have increased every year since 1938. These indices measure the basic strength of the underlying growth forces that have tied California's economic development to the urban-industrial age.

A brief empirical summary of the economic expansion since 1940 provides objective verification of the state's economic capacity to finance state-local expenditures:

CIVILIAN EMPLOYMENT. Employment expanded from a level of 2.7 million in 1940 to 4.2 million in 1950 and 6.9 million in 1965. After several years of difficult readjustment in the aerospace and defense industries, employment reached an all-time high in 1965. In fact, 220,-000 new jobs were added to California's employment base in that year.

PERSONAL INCOME. In 1929, personal income in California reached an historical high of $5.5 billion. During the depression year of 1933, income declined to $3.2 billion. By 1940, as the state stepped over the threshold of the new urban-industrial era, personal income had recovered to a level of $5.8 billion. The postwar period brought a dramatic expansion in income to $19.6 billion in 1950 and $43.4 billion in 1960. Personal income in California reached a level of $60.0 billion in 1965 and will exceed $62.0 billion in 1966. Even when adjusted for the inflation since 1940, the increase in real personal income is impressive.

TAXABLE RETAIL SALES. Testimony to the consumer's confidence in the California economy is the expansion of taxable retail sales from $3.3 billion in 1940 to $23.4 billion in 1960. Taxable retail sales were in excess of $31.0 billion in 1965.

MANUFACTURING EMPLOYMENT. One of the most significant economic developments in California during the past several decades has been the accelerated expansion in the industrial base of the economy. Between 1940 and 1965, manufacturing employment increased by *over* one million from 451,000 in 1940 to 1,500,000 in 1965.

Further insight into the nature of the economic base supporting the state's economy can be gained by an analysis of the distribution of employment between basic and non-basic industries. Basic employment is defined to include agriculture, mineral extraction, and manufacturing; non-basic employment includes construction, transportation, communication, utilities, trade, finance, insurance, real estate, services, and government.

Table 3. Civilian employment in California 1940, 1960, 1965 (thousands)

Basic employment	1940	% of total em- ployment	1960	% of total em- ployment	1965	% of total em- ployment
Agriculture, forestry and fisheries.........	317	11.7%	457	7.6%	361	5.2%
Mineral extraction......	46	.8	33	.6	32	0.3
Manufacturing.........	461	17.0	1,362	22.5	1,500	21.5
Total basic employ- ment...............	824	29.5	1,852	30.7	1,893	27.0
Non-basic employment						
Construction...........	128	4.7	362	6.0	433	6.2
Transportation, com- munication, utilities....	199	7.4	375	6.2	410	5.9
Trade................	659	24.4	1,295	21.4	1,480	21.2
Finance, insurance, real estate..............	124	4.6	285	4.7	360	5.2
Services..............	503	18.6	1,014	16.7	1,312	18.9
Government...........	266	9.8	868	14.3	1,092	15.6
Total non-basic em- ployment...........	1,879	70.5	4,199	69.3	5,087	73.0
Total employment.......	2,703	100.0	6,051	100.0	6,980	100.0

Source: State of California, Department of Industrial Relations.

Examination of the 1940 and 1965 employment patterns reveals an increase in the relative importance of basic industrial employment. Between 1940 and 1960, basic manufacturing employment increased at a more rapid rate than non-basic lines. Since 1960, employment in non-basic lines, particularly in services and government, has increased at a

Financing California government

relatively higher rate. This has helped to close the gap in non-basic employment and output that had developed in the period of rapid urbanization since 1945. It also reflected the net loss of 45,000 jobs in the aerospace industries which was compensated in part by the creation of new jobs in market-oriented manufacturing lines of production.

The foregoing analysis clearly indicates that, when measured in terms of such economic indices as the level of personal income, employment, and retail sales, the California economy demonstrates the capacity to underwrite the public costs of growth.

Fiscal implications of California's pattern of urbanization

A modern system of state-local taxation must be developed within the framework of the urbanization which accompanies rapid population growth. The fiscal ground rules of an agrarian economy are totally inadequate for the financial needs of the public sector of an economy dominated by urbanization and industrial development. It is important, therefore, to review some of the explicit fiscal implications of urban growth.

It is a simple fact that an urban-industrial society places increased expenditure responsibilities on state and local units of government. The typical family farm of three decades ago was a relatively self-contained economic and community unit. Each farm had its own independent water system, waste disposal system, and techniques of police and fire protection. On the other hand, when millions of people are brought together in urban complexes under a low-density land use pattern, the service demands on local and state governments increase at a compound rate. Each new household unit creates a demand for classroom space, water and sewage disposal, police and fire protection, and parks and recreation. Traditionally, local and state units of government have assumed the primary responsibility for providing these services. Urbanization, per se, will increase the role of state and local government if the goal of orderly social and economic development is to be attained.

The pattern of urbanization also carries important fiscal implications. California's growing population is accommodated in the main under a low-density land use pattern.[2] Most citizens prefer to live in single-family dwellings; the automobile has emerged as the most convenient mode of mass transit. A low-density pattern of land usage, which produces a wide geographic dispersion of people, commerce, industry, and communities, is costly insofar as the provision of public goods and services is concerned. Police and fire protection must be extended over a wider area; water, sewer, and utility systems must extend in ever-broadening scope to the outer reaches of the urban complex.

One of the natural outgrowths of the low-density land use pattern which typifies the California growth scene is the emergence of gigantic urban complexes. By the mid-1960's, the geographic outlines of the Bay Area metropolis of 4.0 million persons, and the Southern California metropolis of 11.0 million persons, were well formed.

Because of the unrelenting forces of urbanization, the comfortable citrus, walnut, and apricot "moats" that insulated one community from another during the 1940's are fast disappearing. Each community must now assume that it will become an integral part of a greater urban complex.

The importance of recognizing the place of each community within the greater metropolitan complex is directly related to the fact that most of the problems of a rapidly growing urban area, e.g., air pollution, traffic congestion, inadequate police and fire protection, extend beyond the geographic confines of a given legal jurisdiction. This suggests that the policy framework for coping with taxation and spending problems of local government must be based on the concept of the metropolitan complex. The high degree of fragmentation in local government spending and financing patterns that was compatible with the agricultural way of life is no longer workable.

Local units of government must develop and implement "logical areas of cooperation" along functional lines. In other words, both the expenditure and taxation patterns of local government must be broadened to be geographically commensurate with the emerging metropolitan complexes of the state. The reapportionment program of 1965 may indeed provide the political framework within which a modern state-

[2] In the urbanized area of Southern California, for every ten-person increase in population, one acre of open space is urbanized or converted to residential, industrial, commercial, and civic uses.

local fiscal system can be effected. High priority must attach to this development, as the social and economic costs of delaying solutions to such problems as air pollution are too great to be tolerated.

We should recognize, then, that the process of rapid urbanization, basically a result of population growth, does produce many dilemmas in the arena of state-local finance. There is, first, the inherent conflict between the individual and the community interest. The individual's direct interest will be served by minimizing his tax burdens; the community's interest is promoted by an adequate tax system. For example, students of public finance generally agree that the property tax is inadequate to meet new fiscal requirements for orderly urban and industrial growth. However, changes in the local tax system that would link the revenue-generating capacities of local government more closely to the expanding economic base have failed to gain political passage. The lack of social cohesiveness that is characteristic of an urban complex in which the majority of citizens are newcomers and are culturally diverse militates against natural groundswell of public opinion in favor of a strengthened tax system. The problems of financing the costs of growth are further compounded by the ambivalent attitude of most citizens toward government's role. The typical householder demands the highest quality of services from his community; at the same time he expresses his strenuous objection to tax increases or bond overrides. This ambivalence is strongest at the local level of government.

The economist defines it his duty to point out that an inadequate state-local revenue system produces a disequilibrium in the effective demand and supply relationships of public goods. The disequilibrium manifests itself in many familiar ways: air pollution, traffic congestion, double sessions in schools, inadequate police and fire protection, overcrowded recreation areas, waste disposal problems, underpaid public servants, and social disorder and economic decline in urban core areas. The state of California must begin to apply more rational, objective, and scientific programs of action in the sphere of public finance if the problems of urbanization are to be met.

Conclusions

As we face the fiscal problems of state and local government in California, and attempt to develop solutions for them, we must realize that California is a relatively young economy, in the early stages of economic growth. The rapid population and economic growth of the past two decades may obscure this fact. There are many years of economic growth and urbanization before us, and the problems attendant upon this growth will not diminish. By the mid-1960's, California had reached only one-quarter of its ultimate economic development.

California, in other words, has just begun to realize its economic potential. We must, accordingly, plan wisely for the future in order that this economic potential will in fact be realized. Among other things, this will require the implementation of a public finance policy at the state and local levels equal to the task of striking a tolerable social balance between the supply of private and public goods. It is an inescapable conclusion that the realization of our economic potential depends upon orderly growth, which depends upon an adequate supply of public goods and services, which, in turn, depends upon an adequate state-local revenue system, which, itself, depends upon the income and production base of the state economic system. The apparent circularity of the argument does not vitiate it; on the contrary, it merely supports the position that the economic growth of the private sector of the economy is inextricably tied to the revenue-generating capacity of the public sector's fiscal system. There is no contradiction in suggesting that economic growth depends upon an adequate tax system which, in turn, depends upon economic growth. The true paradox in the relationship between economic development and the system of taxation is philosophical, not economic, in its essence. But even the philosophical dimensions of the arguments against an adequate revenue system are structured on a set of value contradictions which are grounded more on fallacy than on truth. Most of these arguments are based upon a set of social value absolutes, and prove untenable if orderly community and economic growth are indeed to be realized.

Financing local government
in California

An eminent and powerful structure of local government is a basic ingredient of a society which seeks to give to the individual the fullest possible freedom and responsibility.
—*George J. Stigler*

The analysis of the fiscal role of California local government will center around the facts, the priority problem areas, and the leading social policy implications of local finance in the state in the 1960's. Local autonomy is an important attribute of a democratic system of government and is highly dependent upon the maintenance of an adequate system of local taxation. Local taxation allows autonomy of decision-making and fiscal control at the grass-roots level where individual citizens can participate actively in the day-to-day problems of modern government.

One cannot, without contradiction, argue for the preservation of local autonomy while at the same time refusing to lead the way toward improving the fiscal adequacy of the local tax system. Effective local autonomy and fiscal adequacy go hand-in-hand; they are not separable.

Yet, in fact, it is highly probable that local autonomy has been weakened by the failure to maintain an adequate local revenue system. Unfortunately, the annals of fiscal history record few, if any, revolutionary developments in local public finance. On the contrary, the revenue structure of local government tends to be tradition-bound. Changes come by a slow, evolutionary process, generally under conditions of economic stress or other crises such as the property tax assessment scandals in California which made the news during 1965.

The historical failure to adapt the system of local taxation to the needs of an urban-industrial society is consistent with the familiar maxim that "an old tax is a good tax." In other words, local government has not chosen to rock the fiscal boat. Out of deference to tradition, California's local units of government are relying upon a horse-and-buggy tax system to meet the needs of the jet-atomic-electronics-space age. It is not totally surprising, therefore, that local autonomy has been undermined during the past several decades. This decline may be traced, at least in part, to the failure of local government to assume the fiscal responsibilities inherent in the urban-industrial age.

The pattern of local spending in California

Total local "general fund" spending on current operating items and capital outlays was in excess of $6.0 billion in fiscal year 1965.[1] Comparable expenditures totalled $2.3 billion in 1954. When related to the level of state personal income, Californians were allocating 10.7 percent of their current income to finance local expenditures in 1965. This is contrasted with the 8.4 percent of personal income dedicated to school districts, counties, cities, and special districts in 1954. The relative increase in local spending in relation to personal income stands as empirical testimony to the inevitable public costs of urban growth.

During fiscal year 1963, school districts accounted for 38.28 percent of total local spending. County government was second with 30.98 percent, followed by cities with 20.18 percent and special districts with 10.56 percent. In the decade from 1954 to 1963, school district and special district spending increased relatively while the percentage of county and municipal expenditures declined. The increased spending on education was related to ever-expanding enrollments; increased special district spending is explained in the main by the increased number of special districts created during the decade. See Figures 1 and 2.

It is important to examine the specific expenditure profile of each area of local government. School districts carry the basic responsibility of providing a high-quality educational experience for all members of the society regardless of race, creed, socio-economic status, or geo-

---

[1] This figure excludes capital outlays of local government financed through new bond flotations.

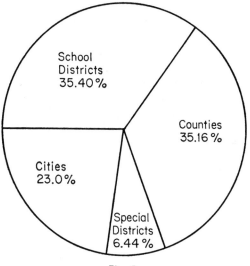

Fig. 1

graphic location. Recent studies of economic productivity have indicated the paramount importance of education in advancing the real standard of living of individuals as well as the total society. In fiscal year 1963, California's school districts spent $2.1 billion. In other

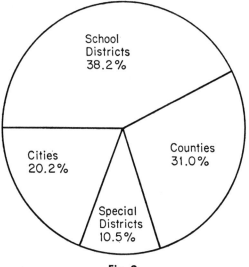

Fig. 2

Table 4.   Local government spending in California fiscal 1954 and 1963

Local unit	1954		1963	
	Spending	% of total	Spending	% of total
School districts	$ 803,378,311	35.40	$2,106,876,881	38.28
Counties	798,128,253	35.16	1,704,606,150	30.98
Cities	522,151,078	23.0	1,110,381,497	20.18
Special districts	146,082,153	6.44	581,027,689	10.56
Total	$2,269,739,795	100.00	$5,502,892,217	100.00
Total local spending as a percent of state personal income	8.4%		10.2%	

Source: Report of the Senate Fact Finding Committee on Revenue and Taxation, *Property Taxes and Other Local Revenue Sources*, Senate of the State of California, March 1965, p. 20.

words, Californians invest about 4.0 cents out of each dollar of personal income to finance a public education program for 4.0 million young people in the grade-range from kindergarten to junior college. From the point of view of the total social and economic benefits derived, this is perhaps one of the wisest expenditures Californians make.

Of the $1.7 billion spent by California counties in 1963, nearly 58.0 percent was channeled into spending on charities and corrections.

Table 5.   School district expenditures in California fiscal 1954 and 1963

Function	1954		1963	
	Amount	% of total	Amount	% of total
Current expenses	$686,551,727	85.46	$1,844,886,566	87.56
Capital outlays *	55,192,416	6.87	58,954,910	2.86
Debt service	61,634,168	7.67	203,035,405	9.61
Total	$803,378,311	100.0	$2,106,876,881	100.0

* Financed by general revenues
Source: Report of the Senate Fact Finding Committee on Revenue and Taxation, *Property Taxes and Other Local Revenue Sources*, Senate of the State of California, March 1965, p. 20.

Poverty and crime are paradoxes of the affluent society; county government in California has traditionally assumed the major responsibilities for providing social remedies in these areas. As indicated in Table 6, county governments provide a system of police and fire protection in the unincorporated areas of the state, and also make sizeable expenditures to promote the health, sanitation, and recreation standards of the citizenry.

California's cities spent over $1.0 billion in fiscal year 1963. Over 50.0 percent of the expenditures were dedicated to provide police and fire protection, health, sanitation, and recreation services to citizens

Table 6. County expenditures in California fiscal 1954 and 1963

Function	1954		1963	
	Amount	% of total	Amount	% of total
General government	$132,169,622	16.56	$ 327,576,785	19.21
Protection	57,588,604	7.21	142,380,969	8.35
Health, sanitation, recreation, education	40,520,436	5.08	93,157,353	5.47
Highways	80,799,624	10.12	136,632,027	8.02
Charities and corrections	484,971,590	60.76	987,819,095	57.95
Debt service	2,078,407	0.26	17,039,921	1.00
Total	$798,128,283	100.0	$1,704,606,150	100.0

Source: Report of the Senate Fact Finding Committee on Revenue and Taxation, *Property Taxes and Other Local Revenue Sources*, Senate of the State of California, March 1965, p. 21.

living in incorporated areas. Californians sacrifice about 2.0 cents out of each dollar of personal income to realize the host of services provided by incorporated cities.

As previously indicated, special districts have come to play a more important role during the past decade. These are more or less autonomous units of local government organized to perform specific functions beyond the legal scope or geographic boundaries of other local jurisdictions. Special districts provide a variety of goods and services, including air pollution control, public transportation, water, flood control, street lighting, hospital and library services, sewage disposal, and storm drain-

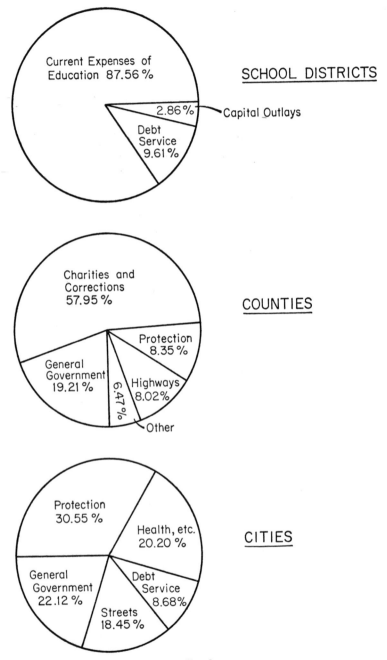

Fig. 3

Table 7. City expenditures in California fiscal 1954 and 1963

| | 1954 | | 1963 | |
Function	Amount	% of total	Amount	% of total
General government	$108,950,305	20.87	$ 245,567,910	22.12
Protection	165,051,115	31.61	339,206,054	30.55
Health, sanitation, recreation, and education	101,543,168	19.45	224,347,014	20.20
Streets	83,296,838	15.95	204,897,753	18.45
Debt services	63,309,652	12.12	96,362,766	8.68
Total	$522,151,078	100.0	$1,110,381,497	100.0

Source: Report of the Senate Fact Finding Committee on Revenue and Taxation, *Property Taxes and Other Local Revenue Sources,* Senate of the State of California, March 1965, p. 22.

age. The special district device has created a type of fiscal release valve at the local level, during a period of rapid urbanization, by providing a means of financing local expenditures when other units of local government have reached legal limits of taxation and bonded indebtedness. Unfortunately, special districts have not been created in every instance to promote the community interest. At times the special district privilege has been abused by developers promoting community concepts that had little or no economic basis for existence. Properly implemented, the

Table 8. Special district expenditures in California fiscal 1954 and 1963

| | 1954 | | 1963 | |
Function	Amount	% of total	Amount	% of total
Operations, maintenance and general expenditures	$ 66,833,427	45.75	$298,045,841	51.30
Capital outlay	42,426,096	29.04	173,860,265	29.92
Debt service	35,822,630	25.21	109,121,583	18.78
Total	$145,082,153	100.0	$581,027,689	100.0

Source: Report of the Senate Fact Finding Committee on Revenue and Taxation, *Property Taxes and Other Local Revenue Sources,* Senate of the State of California, March 1965, p. 23.

2. **Financing local government in California**

special district can play an important role in providing public services, e.g., mass transportation, within the context of a total urban complex, thus avoiding the fragmented approach which results when individual cities and/or counties attempt to provide a specific service which more properly should be uniformly provided on a metropolitan-wide basis. In the decade from 1954 to 1963, there was nearly a fourfold increase in special district expenditures in California.

Local revenue sources in California

Local units of government—school districts, counties, cities, and special districts—received $5.6 billion in revenue from all sources during fiscal year 1963. These revenues are made up of locally-levied taxes, mainly property and sales, state apportionments to school districts, state subventions, shared revenues, e.g., motor vehicle fuel taxes, fees and charges, and other miscellaneous revenues. Locally generated revenues currently account for 70.0 percent of receipts.

The *ad valorem* property tax continues its traditional role as the fiscal foundation of the local revenue system in California. In fiscal 1963, the property tax yielded 45.8 percent of all local *revenues,* and 88.0 percent of locally-generated taxes. The local finance pattern of the

Table 9. **Revenue of local government in California, by source 1930 and 1963**
(millions of dollars)

Revenue source	1930		1963	
	Amount	% of total	Amount	% of total
Property taxes	$351.6	78.8	2,672.5	45.8
Sales taxes	—	—	261.3	6.5
Other revenue	47.4	10.6	995.8	17.7
Grants-in-aid and shared revenues	47.5*	10.6	946.8	16.8
State apportionments to school districts	—	—	744.7	13.2
Total revenue	$446.5	100.0	$5,621.1	100.0

* Includes state subventions to school districts.
Source: State Controller, *Annual Reports.*

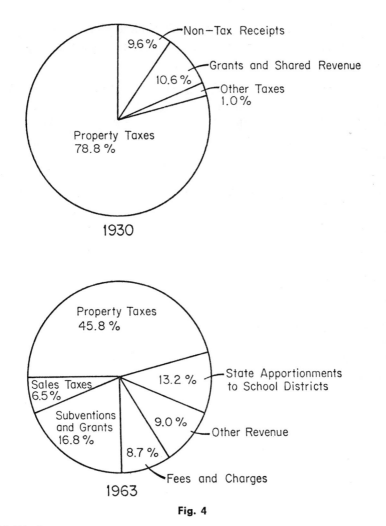

Fig. 4

1960's is contrasted with that of 1930 when the property tax yielded nearly 80.0 percent of all local revenues and almost 99.0 percent of local taxes. The decline in the *relative* importance of the property tax represents one of the few positive developments in California local finance during the past several decades. See Figure 4.

The system of finance varies within the several jurisdictions of local government. It is useful, therefore, to review the revenue structure and recent trends in finance in California's school districts, cities, counties, and special districts. Insofar as each unit of local government is experiencing different pressures on the expenditure side, each is subject to varying problems in the revenue sphere.

SCHOOL DISTRICT FINANCE. In 1930, California's school districts realized 78.2 percent of all revenues through local property taxation. The depression decade of the 1930's demonstrated the limitations of the property tax, and by 1954, 43.5 percent of school district revenues were provided by state apportionments under the "equalization" program formally introduced at the elementary level by statute in 1945. Subsequent to 1954, state apportionments declined relatively. By 1963 they accounted for 34.0 percent of total school district revenues. During the same period, property taxes assumed a greater absolute and relative fiscal responsibility, increasing from 52.0 to 60.0 percent of school district receipts. The implications of this recent trend in local finance will be discussed later.

MUNICIPAL FINANCE. Property taxes have historically provided the main source of revenue for California's cities. In 1930, 96.0 percent of all *tax* receipts and 78.2 percent of total revenues were derived from this source. With the passage of time, cities have sought other sources of local revenue; their entry into the sales tax field in 1945 represents the most significant recent development in municipal finance. By 1963,

Table 10. Sources of school district revenue in California fiscal 1954 and 1963

Revenue source	1954		1963	
	Amount	% of total	Amount	% of total
Property taxes	$430,427,777	52.04	$1,312,718,918	59.92
State apportion-ments	359,505,415	43.47	744,713,165	33.99
Other revenues	37,137,865	4.49	133,232,006	6.08
Total revenue	$827,071,057	100.0	$2,190,664,089	100.0

Source: Report of the Senate Fact Finding Committee on Revenue and Taxation, *Property Taxes and Other Local Revenue Sources,* Senate of the State of California, March 1965, p. 32.

Financing California government

over 19.0 percent of all city revenues were traceable to the sales and use tax; in that year, property taxes accounted for 38.3 percent of the receipts of California's cities.

COUNTY FINANCE. Consistent with the general pattern of local finance in the United States, county units of government relied upon the property tax to yield 100.0 percent of tax revenues and 76.5 percent of total receipts in 1930. In the past several decades greater reliance has been placed upon grants and shared revenues. The latter sources of finance peaked in relative importance in 1954, accounting for 52.7 percent of county revenues. Since that time, property taxes, fees and charges, and sales taxes have increased in relative importance. The Bradley-Burns Uniform Sales and Use Tax Law made a new source of taxation available to counties. This option was exercised for the first time in 1956–1957, and sales and use taxes brought $21.0 million in new revenue to California's counties. In recent years, county sales and use tax proceeds have been approaching $40.0 million.

SPECIAL DISTRICT FINANCE. In 1930, 100 percent of all special district functions were financed by the property tax. Subsequently, there has been a pronounced trend toward the use of service charges in the field of special district finance. In 1963, over 47.0 percent of all

Table 11. Sources of city revenue in California fiscal 1954 and 1963

Revenue source	1954		1963	
	Amount	% of total	Amount	% of total
Property taxes	$216,874,551	44.02	$ 446,581,695	38.33
Subventions and grants	89,039,122	18.07	146,218,523	12.55
Sales tax	49,729,477	10.09	223,382,435	19.17
Fees and charges	37,050,071	7.52	108,377,001	9.30
Other revenue	99,972,785	20.29	240,492,173	20.64
Total revenue	$492,666,006	100.0	$1,165,051,827	100.0

Source: Report of the Senate Fact Finding Committee on Revenue and Taxation, *Property Taxes and Other Local Revenue Sources*, Senate of the State of California, March 1965, p. 29.

Table 12. Sources of county revenue in California fiscal 1954 and 1963

Revenue source	1954 Amount	1954 % of total	1963 Amount	1963 % of total
Property taxes	$302,079,723	38.48	$ 687,961,365	40.16
Subventions and grants	413,569,814	52.69	784,452,541	45.79
Sales tax	—	—	37,974,606	2.22
Fees and charges	33,614,070	4.28	119,955,690	7.00
Other revenue	35,722,090	4.55	82,886,077	4.84
Total	$784,985,697	100.0	$1,713,230,279	100.0

Source: Report of the Senate Fact Finding Committee on Revenue and Taxation, *Property Taxes and Other Local Revenue Sources,* Senate of the State of California, March 1965, p. 28.

revenues were derived from a system of service charges. In the same year, slightly over 40.0 percent of special district revenues were tied to a property tax base.

The preceding summary illustrates the quantitative and qualitative differences in the finance structure of cities, school districts, counties and special districts in California. The data support the conclusion that the importance of the local property tax has declined since the 1930's. They do indicate, however, that a crucial counter-trend has developed in

Table 13. Sources of special district revenue in California fiscal 1954 and 1963

Revenue source	1954 Amount	1954 % of total	1963 Amount	1963 % of total
Property taxes	$ 86,876,499	55.29	$225,232,742	40.79
Subventions and grants	6,252,546	3.98	16,113,781	2.92
Service charges	54,951,541	34.97	261,639,614	47.38
Other revenues	9,048,455	5.76	49,192,625	8.91
Total revenue	$157,129,041	100.0	$552,178,762	100.0

Source: Report of the Senate Fact Finding Committee on Revenue and Taxation, *Property Taxes and Other Local Revenue Sources,* Senate of the State of California, March 1965, p. 31.

county and school district finance during the past decade. In the case of these two local jurisdictions, property taxation has moved against the historical fiscal trend, increasing in both relative and absolute importance. This trend may very well lead to a critical examination of the appropriate place of the property tax in the revenue system of local government in California's rapidly-expanding metropolitan complexes.

The local property tax: a case study in fiscal obsolescence

The leading issue in public finance in the United States is concerned with the future role of the property tax. This form of taxation has been an integral part of state-local revenue systems from time immemorial. Despite the decline in its relative importance during the past several decades, the property tax continues to provide the greatest single source of revenue to California state-local governments combined. One can discern, however, a general groundswell of concern over many of the social, fiscal, and economic effects of the tax. As suggested earlier, the time for critical appraisal has arrived; we may in fact witness an unprecedented fiscal revolution at the local level of government in California in 1966 in the form of drastic revisions in the administration and fiscal role of the property tax. In order to give further impetus to this long overdue revolutionary change in California's local system of taxation, a general critique of the property tax as a source of finance in an urban-industrial society is developed here.

Most students of taxation agree that the burdens of the property tax are distributed in inequitable fashion, that the tax is extremely cumbersome to administer, that it has severe limitations as a fiscal device under rapid urban growth conditions, and that the tax produces undesirable economic resource allocation effects.[2]

Concerning the inequitable manner in which property tax burdens are distributed among economic units of varying wealth and income position, the following considerations are directly relevant to any program of tax reform: First, the property tax is highly discriminatory in its

[2] For a more comprehensive analysis of the property tax in California, see Claremont Social Research Center, *California Local Finance,* (Stanford: Stanford University Press, 1960), pp. 174–204.

application to different forms of wealth as a result of the existing system of classification and exemptions. The greatest burden of the tax falls upon the owner of real property and improvements. The family residence, in particular, makes up a large part of the property tax base. Other forms of wealth such as notes receivable, shares of stock, bonds, mortgages, and deeds of trust, are excluded from the tax base. In other words, we currently exempt from the property tax base those specific forms of wealth where the greatest ability to pay taxes is actually found. There is little social justification for this.

The property tax is also discriminatory in terms of its treatment of real versus personal property. Personal property of considerable value escapes assessment, whereas most real property appears on assessment rolls. It has been suggested that personal property be exempted from taxation in order to eliminate this form of discrimination. This would be unwise for several reasons: First, personal property accounts for nearly 20 percent of county-assessed tangible property in California. Local units of government clearly cannot afford to relinquish such a large part of the property tax base. Second, the discriminatory effects of personal property taxation can be mitigated by a program of improved administration.

No single rationale governs the other exemptions from the property tax base. The $100 exemption for household furnishings, for example, is based on administrative expediency. The veteran's exemption represents a reward for services, and is in lieu of a direct bonus payment. Federal property is exempt under the "immunity doctrine." The exemption of religious, charitable, educational, and social service organizations is attributed to the fact that these institutions perform socially valuable services which would otherwise have to be performed by government at the taxpayer's expense. Unquestionably, many of these exemptions have merit. One cannot ignore the fact, however, that certain exemptions are not grounded upon a socially-oriented rationale, but are simply the result of the pressures of interest groups.

Aside from the inequities which emerge from the assessment process, the proportional general property tax tends to be highly regressive when related to the *incomes* of persons bearing the burden of the tax as such. Thus, although the tax is proportional, per the statute, in relation to the tax base—assessed value—it places a disproportionate burden on lower income groups, many of whom are of retirement age.

The author's sample study of the distribution pattern of property tax burdens in Los Angeles County in 1959 revealed that family units with an annual income of $3,000 or less allocated nearly 7.0 percent of their income to property tax payments; the family unit in the $12,000-to-$14,000 income range, by contrast, was committed to contribute 3.2 percent of its income to property taxes. The regressivity features of the property tax represent the grossest example of injustice in taxation in the affluent society. Further implications of the burden distribution aspects of the property tax will be pursued in Chapter 5. See Figure 5.

The general property tax is not only highly regressive, it also places an inordinately heavy burden upon individuals with limited money income. This is particularly true of retired persons. Since the tax burden is calculated on an *ad valorem* base, the legal tax liability bears little, if any, relationship to the current income of the taxpayer. The tax flagrantly violates the ability-to-pay principle of taxation.

The original objective of property taxation was to tax those forms of property yielding spendable income to the owner. There was an implicit assumption that an effective means of payment—or ability—was generated by the property against which the tax was levied. For wide areas of the property tax today, however, there exists no effective means of payment generated by the property subject to taxation. The tax on residential property falls in the main on non-property sources of income, namely, wages and salaries. For all practical purposes, the property tax liability, though measured against a property base, becomes in large part a tax on non-property income. These latter sources of income are already generously tapped by income and sales taxes. The assumed relationship between property, its income-generating capacity, and taxpaying ability is more mythical than real. Yet, this assumed relationship is the foundation of the local property tax. The assumption is heroic at best and demands a searching reappraisal of the social equity consequences of the tax.

The administrative complexities inherent in a system of property taxation are well beyond the comprehension of the typical taxpayer. A few statistics will indicate the magnitude of the administrative task

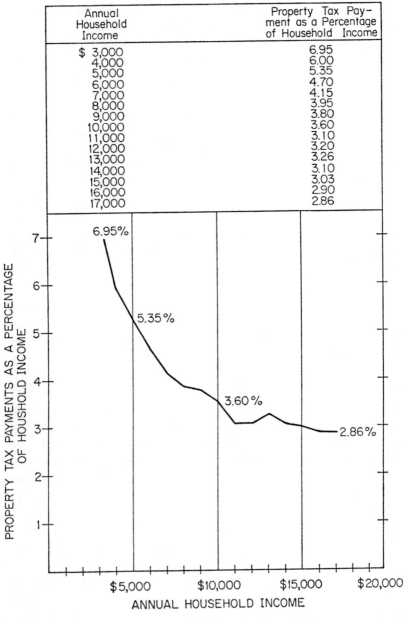

Annual Household Income	Property Tax Payment as a Percentage of Household Income
$ 3,000	6.95
4,000	6.00
5,000	5.35
6,000	4.70
7,000	4.15
8,000	3.95
9,000	3.80
10,000	3.60
11,000	3.10
12,000	3.20
13,000	3.26
14,000	3.10
15,000	3.03
16,000	2.90
17,000	2.86

Fig. 5

confronting the assessor of Los Angeles County: each year the assessor must set down a judgment with respect to the fair and equitable assessed value of 1,800,000 parcels of real estate, a quarter of a million businesses, more than 70,000 boats and 4,000 airplanes. The assessor must stay abreast of the market value information surrounding some 200,000 real estate transactions; over 300,000 veteran exemptions and several thousand welfare and church exemption claims must be reviewed and processed annually. To handle this task over seven and one-half million pieces of paper are handled each year.[3] There must be an easier way!

Professionals who spend their working lives in the field of valuation will attest to the incredible complexities and resultant subjectivity associated with the process of assigning a "fair market value" to a property right. Even at its best, the assessment process will work inequities as between different parcels and types of property; geographic differences in assessment ratios are a matter of public record. The end result is inequity in the distribution of property tax burdens.[4] The administrative complexities surrounding the property tax provide one very good reason for a gradual movement away from this form of taxation.

The existing system of property taxation creates many perverse and irrational social and economic consequences that an urban-industrial society can no longer afford to ignore. Witness the distortions in commercial and industrial inventory practices resulting from the legal requirement that the tax lien date is the first Monday in March; witness, further, the incorporation of islands of wealth variously referred to as cities of industry, commerce, and dairies; witness the futile attempts of individual local jurisdictions to achieve "balanced land usage" in order to alleviate the pressures on the property tax base. Visualize, if you will, the patchwork pattern of commercial and industrial land use in our

[3] Release from Los Angeles County Assessor, Philip E. Watson, "Economy and Efficiency," 1965. Mr. Watson favors the enactment of legislation to limit the amount of property taxes anyone would have to pay to 2 percent of market value. This would have the effect of placing the primary responsibility for *changes* in property tax burdens on county boards of supervisors, school board trustees, and city councils. These latter groups establish the actual tax rate per $100 of assessed valuation.
[4] Recent developments in California reveal that certain properties can indeed escape their fair share of the burden through the process of arbitrarily scaling down valuations.

emerging urban complexes, a direct consequence of the local property tax. Finally, witness the artificial pressures for the conversion of valuable open space to urban use on lands contiguous to areas of rapid population growth and economic development.[5] One can cite instances in which assessment practices on agricultural lands in California actually vitiate municipal master plan zoning ordinances aimed at preserving community green belt areas. The effects of property taxation on urbanization and economic processes are of such significance that they cannot be ignored. Existing property taxation encourages a pattern of disorderly community and economic growth. Even this cursory review of the perverse socio-economic consequences of the tax should convince the reader that property tax reform must be effected without further delay.

Finally, one further shortcoming of the property tax must be examined, namely, its fiscal limitations under conditions of rapid urban growth. First of all, it should be recognized that the typical single-family dwelling in California does not begin to pay the public costs associated with its existence. Assume that the residence and land has a market value of $20,000 and that the assessed valuation base on the property is set at $5,000. With a tax rate of $10.00 per hundred dollars of assessed valuation the property yields an annual tax revenue of $500 to the school district, city, county, and special districts. In 1962–1963, the current expense of education per pupil in a California elementary school district with 2,000 or more in average daily attendance averaged $385.56. Thus, a household with two children in the elementary school system represents an effective demand for $771.12 in current operating costs of education. This should illustrate the distinct limitations of a property tax which rests to a considerable degree on a residential real property base.

The property tax proves to be fiscally inadequate on several other counts: Although market values of property increase substantially during periods of rapid growth, assessed valuations do not increase at an equal pace. One finds little correlation between the rate of growth of a

[5] For an excellent treatment of this problem see David R. Doerr and Raymond R. Sullivan, "Property Taxation and Land Use," Assembly Interim Committee on Revenue and Taxation, *Taxation of Property in California,* December 1964, pp. 203–228.

community and the rate of increase in the revenue-generating capacity of the property tax. Many times the most rapid growth area may have the least fiscal capacity under a property tax base. Tax consciousness is most evident at the local level of government. This means effective resistance to higher tax rates and assessed valuations; constitutional and statutory provisions limit the financial capacities of local government. As long as these conditions persist, and they appear to be inherent in the process of property taxation, local units of goverment in California will face chronic financial problems. The remedy lies in effecting meaningful innovations in the fiscal structure of local governments.[6]

On the search for new local revenue

In the introductory paragraphs to this chapter reference was made to the importance of local autonomy in the California system of government. It was suggested that local autonomy in government was directly dependent upon an adequate, well-balanced system of taxation. What, then, are local units of government doing to enhance the strength of the local tax system in instances in which discretionary alternatives are available?

In preparing the report of the Senate Fact Finding Committee on Revenue Taxation, *Property Taxes and Other Local Revenue Sources,* the research team, with the cooperation of the League of California Cities, polled all California cities on the question of new revenue sources. Of the 391 cities in the survey, 198 responded. The results give important insights into the attitudes of city administrators and the various avenues of approach being used or considered to remedy the fiscal deficiencies of the local tax system.

With respect to the adequacy of the local property tax, 60.0 percent of the respondents held that the tax would not meet the finance needs of cities during the next 10 years; 21.0 percent felt that the

[6] For instance, eliminating the school district property tax and transferring the total fiscal responsibility for public education to the state of California through extending the sales and use tax to services might be one method of reducing the property tax burden. Another method of overcoming the inequity of penalizing people who improve their property and rewarding those who allow their improvements to fall into deterioration is to fix assessments on the value of land only. While there are complexities involved in both of these proposals, they can be reduced to practical solutions.

property tax would generate sufficient revenues. Over three-fourths of the cities in which public administrators consider the property tax an inadequate revenue source have levied new taxes within the past several years or are now considering new revenue sources.

Interestingly enough, the motel-hotel occupancy tax was most frequently mentioned as a potential source of new revenue. Forty of the cities in the sample had introduced the hotel-motel tax within the past three years; another 50 cities indicated that they were considering the installation of such a tax. Increased business license fees, miscellaneous fees and licenses, and property development taxes also ranked high in consideration as potential sources of new city revenue.

Perhaps the most significant finding of relevance to the fiscal future of California's cities related to the attitude toward the expansion of locally-levied taxes collected by the state. This would involve the extension of the state-local shared tax concept already in effect in the sales and use and highway tax fields. Nearly 44.0 percent of the cities completing the questionnaire favored extension of the state-local shared tax device; 18.7 percent of the cities indicated opposition to this avenue of increased local taxation. Over three-fourths of the cities queried gave

Table 14. Non-property revenue sources under consideration by California cities 1964

Revenue source	Number of cities	Percent of responding cities	
		Unweighted	Weighted by total city revenue*
Business license fees	25	12.6	6.3
Miscellaneous fees and licenses	39	19.7	16.6
Hotel occupancy taxes	50	25.2	16.0
Property development taxes	23	11.6	10.4
Municipal utilities	8	4.0	1.2
Cigarette taxes	13	6.5	12.2
Amusement-admissions taxes	3	1.5	1.1
Income taxes	5	2.5	.8
Other	19	9.5	4.2

* Weighted by total revenue collected by responding cities during 1962–1963.
Source: Report of the Senate Fact Finding Committee on Revenue and Taxation, *Property Taxes and Other Local Revenue Sources*, March 1965, p. 87.

either unqualified or qualified support for expanded use of the state-local shared tax device. In view of the author's belief that the *state-local-shared income tax* holds the key to the fiscal future of local government in California, these findings point the way toward a feasible solution to the financial problems which currently plague school districts, cities, and counties in California.

Table 15. Attitudes of California cities toward increase in locally-levied taxes collected by the state

Question: Would your city generally favor increasing the importance of the role played by tax measures locally levied and state collected, such as the present sales tax arrangement?

| | | Percentage | |
Answer	Number of cities	Unweighted	Weighted by total city revenue*
No	37	18.7	6.6
Yes, unqualified	87	43.9	50.9
Yes, but with qualification	34	17.2	8.3
Yes, but only on specific items	12	6.1	27.7
No answer	28	14.1	6.5
Total	198	100.0	100.0

* Weighted by total revenue collected by responding cities during 1962–1963.
Source: Report of the Senate Fact Finding Committee on Revenue and Taxation, *Property Taxes and Other Local Revenue Sources,* March 1965, p. 88.

The California state
fiscal system

> The dynamics of the new technology are placing great new
> stresses on state and local finance. Rapid technological
> advance means that what we begin today may be obsolescent
> before completed, whether it be a rapid transit system, an
> airport, a freeway, a sewage system or a textbook.
> —*Governor Edmund G. Brown*

3

The profile of public finance at the state level in California is in striking contrast with that of local government. This chapter attempts to place into focus the salient facts, priority problem areas, and social policy implications of state finance in California in the 1960's.

Recent trends in the overall fiscal system

The California fiscal system will be described and analyzed in terms of four categories of finance: (1) general fund revenues, (2) motor vehicle revenues, (3) federal grant-in-aid revenues, and (4) general obligation bonds.

The social policy issue of federal aid to lower levels of government has been the subject of considerable debate during the past several decades. The fiscal facts of current state finance in California suggest that the issue is now of purely academic interest. The growth in the relative and absolute importance of federal aid within recent years has been a fiscal revolution at the state-local level in California.

A review of the total revenue profile of the state in 1964 reveals that of the $4.5 billion in disposable funds produced by taxes (general fund and highway), intergovernmental grants, and miscellaneous sources, over $1.17 billion (25.8 percent) was realized in the form

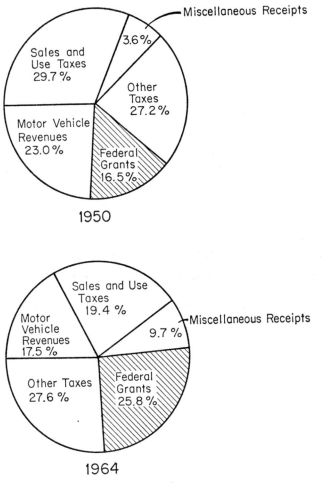

1950

1964

Fig. 6

of federal grants-in-aid. In 1950, federal grants-in-aid to the state of California amounted to $179.0 million, representing 16.5 percent of total revenues. See Figure 6.

Here, then, is empirical evidence of a recent revolutionary development in California finance. The increasing role of the federal government can best be described as a case history in fiscal default on the part of state and local units of government. The conservative views this default with pain. The liberal looks upon it with pleasure. However, it would appear that the federal government's role in state and local finance will continue to expand, partly as a result of the social programs which make up the fabric of the Great Society. Certainly there will be no reversal of this trend in public finance until state and local revenue systems are strengthened.

General fund revenues

Despite the recent growth in federal grants-in-aid, the general fund represents the central core of California's system of finance. Revenues to the state general fund accrue from a variety of broadly based taxes and miscellaneous sources. A 3.0 percent sales and use tax provided nearly 42.0 percent of the $2.24 billion general fund revenues collected by the state in fiscal year 1965. Bank and corporation franchise and income taxes and the personal income tax ranked second and third in order of importance, yielding, respectively, 18.6 and 18.3 percent of 1965 general fund revenues.

The general revenue system of the state is broadly based, characterized by administrative simplicity, and directly correlated in its revenue-raising capabilities with the state's expanding levels of personal and business income, output, spending, and employment. These are all positive attributes of an effective tax system in an urban-industrial age.

The last significant tax legislation in California was passed in 1959. Interim growth pressures make it highly probable that significant changes in the California general fund revenue system will be effected within the next several sessions of the legislature. In view of these prospective changes, only a brief summary of descriptive details relating to the general fund as it existed early in 1966 will be developed.[1]

CALIFORNIA GENERAL FUND CONSUMPTION TAXES. Four consumer-oriented taxes, on retail sales and use, cigarettes, alcoholic beverages and horse racing, provided $1.12 billion—exactly 50.0 percent of all

[1] For a more detailed description, see the excellent studies prepared by the Assembly Interim Committee on Revenue and Taxation and the Senate Fact Finding Committee on Revenue and Taxation during 1964 and 1965. Several of these studies were cited in the preceding chapter. Numerous citations to the series will be made throughout the remainder of this study.

Table 16. California state revenue sources 1950 and 1964
(billions of dollars)

Revenue sources	1950		1964	
	Amount	% of total	Amount	% of total
State taxes	$ .806	79.9	$2.930	64.5
Federal grants-in-aid	.179	16.5	1.172	25.8
Miscellaneous revenues	.098	3.6	.437	9.7
Total	$1.083	100.0	$4.539	100.0

Source: U.S. Department of Commerce, Bureau of Census, *Compendium of State Government Finances.*

general fund revenues—in fiscal year 1965. It is a fact, then, that the California state revenue system is heavily oriented toward household spending.

The state retail sales and use tax is levied at a rate of 3.0 percent on transactions involving tangible personal property. Major exemptions from the tax include food for off-premise consumption, gas, electricity, telephone and telegraph services, water, motor vehicle fuels, newspapers and periodicals, and sales to the federal government. Goods purchased for resale, various intermediary products used in the production of food, and certain sales in interstate and foreign commerce are also exempted. Cities and counties in California also levy a 1.0 percent sales and use tax. Collections are made by the state board of equalization; the proceeds are remitted to local units of government and are divided between county and municipal units in a ratio determined at the local level. State and local retail sales and use taxes provided over $1.3 billion in revenue during fiscal year 1965.

Since 1959, California has taxed cigarettes at a rate of 3 cents per pack. During the first year of its existence the tax generated $64.8 million in revenue for the state. By fiscal year 1964–1965, general fund revenues from the cigarette tax had risen nearly $10.0 million to $74.5 million. An effort to raise the tax to 8 cents per pack failed in the 1965 session of the legislature. It is reasonable to predict that tax levies on tobacco products will increase in the near future.

Table 17. General fund revenues in California 1965

	Total revenue	Percent of total revenue
General tax and license revenues		
Alcoholic beverage revenues—		
Beer and wine excise tax....................$	12,426,372	0.6
Distilled spirits excise tax......................	53,929,987	2.4
Liquor license fees*..........................	3,453,305	0.1
Total alcoholic beverage revenues.............	69,809,664	3.1
Bank and corporation franchise and income taxes.....	416,448,739	18.6
Cigarette tax...................................	74,514,997	3.3
Gift tax..	9,850,774	0.4
Horse racing revenue*..........................	37,897,449	1.7
Inheritance tax.................................	104,877,607	4.7
Insurance companies tax.........................	94,817,325	4.2
Motor vehicle license fees (in lieu tax)..............	1,045,000	...
Personal income tax............................	410,499,044	18.3
Private car tax.................................	2,017,084	0.1
Retail sales and use tax and fees..................	939,267,895	41.9
Total tax and license revenues................	2,161,045,578	96.3
Other revenues		
Royalties and other revenue from state lands*.......	17,006,293	0.8
Penalty assessments on traffic violations	7,267,848	0.3
Interest on investments and treasury deposits.........	24,073,822	1.1
Revenues not otherwise classified..................	34,894,621	1.5
Total other revenues.......................	83,242,584	3.7
Total general fund revenues ....$	2,244,288,162	100.0

* General fund share only.
Source: State Controller, *Annual Report*.

Alcoholic beverage excise taxes and license fees yielded $69.8 million, or 3.1 percent, of state general fund revenue in the period ending June 30, 1965. Of this total, $66.3 million was produced by excises on beer, wine, and distilled spirit purchases. Annual revenues from the system of license fees are in excess of $15.0 million. The largest share of these license fees is returned to the city or county in which the licensed establishment is located. The proceeds from the initial license fees, and 10 percent of renewal fees, are impounded for general fund purposes.

The general fund's share of horse-racing revenues was $37.9 million in fiscal year 1965. In California, 77 percent of the state's share of pari-mutuel receipts is impounded for general fund purposes; 21.0 percent is earmarked for conservation, and another 2.0 percent of the state's share is earmarked for local fairs.[2] Total horse-racing revenues for 1965 are estimated at $45.0 million. In 1952, this source of revenue yielded $20.5 million.[3]

CALIFORNIA GENERAL FUND TAXES ON THE BUSINESS SECTOR. Direct taxes on California business and industry, which accrue to the general fund, yielded $523.3 million, or 22.9 percent of general fund revenue in 1965. Three forms of taxation, the bank and corporation franchise and income, insurance company, and private car, provide the basis for business general fund contributions. Severance taxes on extractive industries yield around $1.2 million each year; part of the motor vehicle license fees of $1.0 million each year also is attributable to the business sector. Severance tax revenues are not available to the general fund. They are earmarked for expenditure on "conservation" programs.

A 1965 report to the Senate Fact Finding Committee on Revenue and Taxation described business income taxation in California along the following lines:

The Bank and Corporation Tax Law as it now exists imposes a tax which may be described in broad terms as a tax based on net income, and the basic rate is 5.5 percent. However, the technical incidence of the tax and the rate incurred differ as to classes of taxpayers.

THE FRANCHISE TAX ON BUSINESS CORPORATIONS

This tax is imposed on corporations doing business in the state, for the privilege of exercising their corporate franchise. The tax is measured by the net income of the preceding year. The rate is 5.5 percent with a minimum tax of $100.

THE FRANCHISE TAX ON BANKS

This tax is imposed on banks located within the limits of the state. It is in lieu of all other taxes and licenses, state, county and local, except taxes on

[2] Tax Foundation, *Earmarked State Taxes,* (New York, 1965) p. 35.
[3] For further details on consumption taxes in California, see the Report of the Senate Fact Finding Committee on Revenue and Taxation, *General Fund Consumption Taxes,* Senate of the State of California, January 1965.

real property. The measure of the tax is the net income of the preceding year calculated to make up for the fact that banks pay no taxes on their personal property. This additional percentage is equal to the percentage of net income which business corporations pay as personal property taxes. The maximum rate is 9.5 percent and there is no minimum tax.

THE FRANCHISE TAX ON FINANCIAL CORPORATIONS

To avoid discrimination, financial corporations (i.e., those in competition with banks) are taxed at the same rate as banks. However, since these corporations are not exempt from personal property or license taxes, they are allowed a credit for such taxes but their tax after the credit must not be less than 5.5 percent of net income or $100, whichever is greater.

THE FRANCHISE TAX ON INACTIVE CORPORATIONS

Every corporation having the right to do business in the state (i.e., domestic corporations and qualified foreign corporations) but not exercising its franchise must pay an annual tax of $100.

THE CORPORATION INCOME TAX

This tax is imposed in those situations where a privilege tax cannot be imposed. Accordingly, it is imposed on corporations doing exclusively interstate business in California, on associations having corporate characteristics but no corporate franchise (e.g., business trusts), and on inactive corporations that receive net income but are not doing business. The tax is a direct net income tax, at a rate of 5.5 percent. The franchise tax and the corporation income tax are mutually exclusive, i.e., a corporation cannot be liable for both taxes for the same period.[4]

The Senate *Report* summarized the taxation of insurance companies in California in the following fashion:

The present pattern of California insurance taxation basically stems from a constitutional amendment adopted in 1910 which levied a uniform tax on gross premiums received from business done in California by both domestic and foreign companies. There have been no significant changes in state insurance taxation since 1948 when the present permanent tax rate of 2.35 percent became effective, together with the provision that insurance tax credits would be limited to the real property taxes paid on the insurance company's home or principal office. In 1963, a tax prepayment schedule was

[4] Report of the Senate Fact Finding Committee on Revenue and Taxation, *Taxes on Business Income,* Senate of the State of California, March 1965, p. 18.

adopted to become effective over the years 1964 to 1967. During this interim period the tax rate has been lowered to 2.33 percent, but is to return automatically to 2.35 percent in 1968.[5]

The private car tax is a special property tax levied on railroad cars owned by private companies. The tax is administered by the State Board of Equilization. General fund revenues from this source averaged around $2.0 million in recent years.[6]

CALIFORNIA GENERAL FUND TAXES ON PERSONAL INCOME. California levies a personal income tax on individuals, fiduciaries, estates, and trusts at rates ranging from 1.0 to 7.0 percent of taxable income. General fund revenue from this source increased from $91.0 million and 8.8 percent of *total state taxes* in fiscal year 1952, to $410 million and 13.1 percent of total tax revenues in 1965.

The legal concept of taxable income in California is roughly comparable to that of the federal income tax. There are exceptions, however. For example, California does not allow for a dividend exclusion; the state exempts up to $1,000 of military compensation on retirement pay; interest on federal and California state-local bond obligations is excluded from the tax base.

Under the personal income tax law in effect in 1966, a married couple filing a joint return was allowed an exemption of $3,000. Single persons were privileged to take an exemption of $1,500, and an allowance of $600 for each dependent was in effect. Personal income tax rates for married couples filing a joint return ranged from 1.0 percent on the first $5,000 of taxable income to 7.0 percent on taxable income of $30,000 and above. The complete tax rate structure is presented in Table 18.

Interstate per capita comparisons suggest that individual income tax burdens under the California state system are not oppressive. In 1963, per capita personal income taxes in California averaged $18.30. This is a nominal burden as revealed by per capita burdens in several other states: Delaware, $76.98; New York, $57.53; Oregon, $54.73;

[5] *Ibid.*, p. 42.
[6] For further details see the Report of the Senate Fact Finding Committee on Revenue and Taxation, *The Private Car Tax,* Senate of the State of California, April 1965.

Wisconsin, $53.87; Alaska, $52.44; Hawaii, $45.49, and Minnesota, $41.31. The per capita average for all states was $25.33 in 1963.[7] Both the business and household sectors are subject to relatively moderate rates of income taxation under existing California statutes.

Table 18. Tax rates under the California personal income tax 1966

Percent-age tax rate	Taxable income	
	Married couple joint return	All other returns
1%	Up to $ 5,000	Up to $ 2,500
2	$ 5,000 – 10,000	$ 2,500 – 5,000
3	10,000 – 15,000	5,000 – 7,500
4	15,000 – 20,000	7,500 – 10,000
5	20,000 – 25,000	10,000 – 12,500
6	25,000 – 30,000	12,500 – 15,000
7	30,000 and over	15,000 and over

Source: State of California, *Revenue and Taxation Code*

CALIFORNIA GENERAL FUND TAXES ON DEATH AND GIFT WEALTH TRANSFERS. During fiscal year 1965 gift and inheritance taxes on transfers of wealth yielded $114.7 million, 5.1 percent, of general fund revenue. In fiscal 1960, these two forms of wealth taxation accounted for $47.2 million, or 3.0 percent of revenue, indicating a moderate increase in the relative importance of gift and inheritance taxes to the general fund in the past several years. It is highly unlikely that taxes on wealth transfers will ever play a major role in financing of California government.[8]

Other revenues to the state general fund are royalties from state lands, penalty assessments on traffic violations, interest on investments

[7] For a more thorough analysis of the individual income tax, see the Report of the Senate Fact Finding Committee on Revenue and Taxation, *The California Personal Income Tax,* Senate of the State of California, January 1965.
[8] Report of the Senate Fact Finding Committee on Revenue and Taxation, *Death and Gift Taxation,* Senate of the State of California, January 1965.

and treasury deposits. These sources provided $83.2 million, 3.7 percent, of 1965 revenues.

**Table 19. State inheritance-gift tax
revenues in California 1936–1965
(thousands of dollars)**

Fiscal year	Tax receipts	Percent of total revenue*
1936	$ 6,687	3.5
1946	14,514	2.8
1956	36,334	2.3
1960	47,189	2.1
1962	72,012	3.0
1964	101,477	3.4
1965	114,727	3.7

*Net budget receipts, including general fund plus motor vehicle revenues.
Source: State Controller, *Annual Reports*.

Earmarked motor vehicle revenues

In the fiscal year ending June 30, 1965, the system of highway use taxes and vehicle license fees yielded revenues of $885.0 million. These receipts are earmarked to finance construction and maintenance of state highways and local roads and streets, licensing of vehicles and drivers, traffic regulation, and enforcement of motor vehicle laws and administration. Since these revenues are earmarked to finance specific functions relating to California's 9 million motor vehicles, they are not available to the general fund.

Over 55.0 percent of the motor vehicle revenues are derived from a 7 cents per gallon tax on gasoline and diesel fuels. All private passenger vehicles are subject to a registration fee; commercial vehicles pay a registration fee as well as a weight fee. For the privilege of operating on public highways an "in lieu" tax based on 2.0 percent of market value is levied on all vehicles. Vehicle operators who transport persons or property pay a tax of 1.5 percent of gross receipts. Drivers' license fees yielded approximately $10.0 million to motor vehicle revenues in fiscal year 1965.

In recent years, at least 45.0 percent of the highway-user taxes and license fees have been apportioned to counties and cities. Most of these revenues are used to finance local street and road improvement and maintenance programs. The various highway-user taxes and fees are levied under the benefit principle of taxation. Under this principle the recipient of a government good or service is expected to pay the cost. The benefits-received principle provides an excellent rationale for financ-

Table 20. Source and disposition of motor vehicle revenues in California 1965

	1964–65 Fiscal Year
REVENUES	
Highway users taxes	
Motor vehicle fuel tax	
Gasoline	$480,003,635
Use (diesel)	28,606,051
Storage tax	1,090,237
Motor vehicle registration, drivers' license fees, and related revenues	180,401,569
Motor vehicle transportation (truck) tax	16,014,463
Miscellaneous highway users tax revenues	930,453
Total highway users tax revenues	707,046,408
Motor vehicle license fees ("in lieu" tax) and related revenues	177,868,423
Total revenues	$884,914,831
DISPOSITION	
State expenditures	
Administration, collection and law enforcement	
Highway Transportation Agency	$ 60,441
Department of Motor Vehicles	42,227,336
Department of California Highway Patrol	46,454,701
Board of Equalization, State Controller, Division of Aeronautics and Golden Gate Commission	3,098,673
Principal and interest on state highway bonds	1,045,000
Total	92,886,151
Transfer to State Highway Fund for—	
Construction, maintenance and administration of state highways	371,267,600
Allocation to local agencies for storm and flood damage repair	308,687
Transfer to Street and Highway Disaster Fund	205,791
Transfer to Small Craft Harbor Revolving Fund	2,000,000
Transfer to Airport Assistance Fund	350,000
Total state expenditures	$467,018,229

Table 20. Source and disposition of motor vehicle revenues in California 1965 (*continued*)

	1964–65 Fiscal Year
Apportionments to counties	
Highway users taxes—for public roads, streets and highways and related purposes	$105,703,843
Highway users taxes—for select system of county roads	20,484,408
Motor vehicle license fees ("in lieu" tax)—for any state purpose	81,201,980
Trailer coach license fees—for distribution, equally between counties, cities and school districts, to be expended for any state purpose	5,946,862
Total apportionments to counties	213,337,093
Apportionments to cities	
Highway users taxes—for city streets and other related purposes	48,543,892
Highway users taxes—for select system of city streets	47,310,312
Motor vehicle license fees—for expenditure on law enforcement, regulation and control and fire protection of highway traffic and for any state purpose	81,201,980
Total apportionments to cities	177,056,184
Total expenditures and apportionments	$857,411,506

Note: Difference between total revenues and total expenditures and apportionments reflects carryover of balances between years.
Source: State Controller, *Annual Reports*.

ing a highway and street system. The user of the highway should expect to pay the costs associated with the construction and operation of the system.[9]

Federal grant-in-aid revenues

An analysis of the revenue system of the state of California would be incomplete in substance and detail if federal grants-in-aid were omitted. Apparently federal grants are now an institutionalized feature of the state's revenue system.

During fiscal year 1964, federal aid payments to the state government exceeded $1.0 billion, accounting for more than one-fourth of total receipts. Federal funds were made available in three major expenditure areas: public welfare, highways, and education. A comparison of the expenditure pattern in 1950 and 1964 is detailed in Table 21.

[9] The Report of the Senate Fact Finding Committee on Revenue and Taxation, *Highway-User Taxes,* Senate of the State of California, June, 1965, is an excellent exposition on motor vehicle taxation in California. Comparisons with other states are included in the study.

Table 21. Federal aid payments to California state government 1950 and 1964 (thousands of dollars)

Aid program	1950	1964
Education	$ 9,547	$ 380,531
Highways	17,349	299,507
Public welfare	128,661	395,836
Old-age assistance		(181,575)
Aid to families with dependent children		(134,028)
Aid to blind		(8,014)
Aid to disabled		(29,094)
Other		(43,125)
Health and hospital	2,103	14,740
Other*	21,368	81,353
	$179,028	$1,171,967

* Natural resources, employment security administration, and miscellaneous grants.
Source: U.S. Department of Commerce, Bureau of Census, *Compendium of State Government Finances.*

The impact of federal grants on the state's system of finance carries many interesting philosophical, social value, political, and economic implications. From all indications, the body politic is reconciled to the expanding role of the federal grant-in-aid program. In terms of promoting the economic welfare of those groups who have been unable to enter the mainstream of affluence, the federal program has great merit. During twenty-five years of unprecedented prosperity the state and local governments have not provided the revenues and programs to bring the "invisible" Americans—the aged, the disabled, the underprivileged—out from under the shadow of poverty.

General bonded indebtedness in California

During the fiscal year 1965, the state's bonded debt increased by $445.0 million to bring the total of outstanding general obligation bonds to $3.4 billion. In a state where population growth and urbanization forces are strong it is neither possible nor desirable to finance all expenditures through general revenue sources. In fact, one might argue that most capital outlays on public facilities (with the exception of streets and highways) should be financed through new bond flotations.

This would have the effect of relieving some of the pressures on the system of taxation and enhance the prospect of financing socially necessary public goods and services of a non-capital nature.

The California general obligation bond program is directed, in the main, toward the financing of several high-priority areas of need: The Cal-vet farm and home loan program provides low-cost financing for qualified veterans; school districts, not otherwise able to provide ade-

Table 22. State of California general obligation bonds June 30, 1965

Expenditure area	Bonds outstanding	Bonds authorized and unissued
State highways..........................$	1,000,000	—
Sacramento state building..................	3,000,000	—
San Francisco state building...............	20,000	—
University of California....................	—	—
State buildings and university buildings........	—	—
California tenth olympiad..................	150,000	—
San Francisco harbor improvement..........	43,739,000	$ 18,197,000
Small craft harbor development............	10,000,000	—
State construction program................	553,400,000	450,000,000
Veterans farm and home building..........	1,290,140,000	250,000,000
State school building aid.................	1,171,400,000	210,000,000
State water bonds.......................	350,000,000	1,400,000,000
Beach, park, recreational, and historical facilities.............................	—	150,000,000
Total bonded debt...............$3,422,849,000		$2,478,197,000
Deduct:		
Self-liquidating bonds		
San Francisco harbor improvement.......$	43,739,000	$ 18,197,000
Small craft harbor development.........	10,000,000	—
Veterans farm and home building.......	1,290,140,000	250,000,000
State water bonds...................	350,000,000	1,400,000,000
Total self-liquidating bonds.........$1,693,879,000		$1,668,197,000
Bonds offset by cash reserves		
California tenth olympiad................$	*134,000	—
Sacramento state building..............	*3,000,000	—
Total sinking funds...............$	3,134,000	—
General fund bonded debt...............$1,725,836,000		$ 810,000,000

* Figures shown represent reserves, not bonds.
Source: State Controller, *Annual Report.*

3. The California state fiscal system

quate physical facilities to accommodate increasing public school enrollments, are assisted under the school-building aid program; the state facility construction program provides underwriting for capital expansion in higher education and other areas. The all-important California Water Plan is being financed by the $1.75 billion general obligation bonds authorized by voters in 1960; harbor improvements, beach, park, recreational, and historical facilities are also funded by bond authorizations.

Of the total general bonded debt outstanding on June 30, 1965, 49.0 percent was self-liquidating. Another 34.0 percent was partially self-liquidating, leaving a net general bonded debt of $1.7 billion. School district reimbursements to the state reduced the debt by another $480 million. General fund revenues, in other words, were committed to service an estimated $1.2 billion of debt in 1965. Per capita state and local net debt in California in 1960 was $342. This compares favorably with New York's per capita state-local indebtedness of $603 in the same year.

Table 23. California state general bond debt 1930–1965 (thousands of dollars)

Year	Total	Year	Total
1930	119,727	1962	2,600,707
1940	261,852	1963	2,706,546
1950	243,400	1964	2,978,210
1960	1,928,705	1965	3,422,849
1961	2,281,217		

Source: State Controller, *Annual Reports.*

Contrasting state systems of taxation: California, New York, and Washington

One of the most intriguing aspects of the state fiscal scene in the United States is the great diversity in tax systems from state to state. The contrasts which exist today stand as testimony to the independence that has governed historical developments in state finance. No single or general concept of the system of revenue appropriate to state governments has held sway. This will be demonstrated in a comparative analysis of the sources of taxation relied upon in California, New York, and Washington.

New York and California state governments each realized $2.5 billion in general fund and motor vehicle revenues in fiscal year 1963. In the case of New York, 40.6 percent ($1.0 billion) of the revenues was provided by the individual income tax; in California, personal income taxes amounted to $322.0 million, representing 12.2 percent of total revenues. The sales and use tax is the leading source of tax revenue in California, providing 31.8 percent of total revenues in 1963.

The state of Washington, by contrast, secured nearly 55.0 percent of its 1963 revenues from the sales and use tax. Neither a personal nor corporate income tax is used in the state's revenue system. The sales and use tax is levied at a 4.0 percent rate on all retail sales including food purchases, personal business or professional services, and retail sales of intoxicants by state liquor stores. There are certain explicit exemptions from the sales tax base. The more important ones are rolling stock, purebred livestock, newspapers, and airplanes in interstate commerce. See Figure 7.

In many respects California has a more balanced state tax system than either New York or Washington. California derives over 56.0 percent of its tax revenues from three major sources: sales and use, and personal and business income taxes. On the other hand, the New York State system of taxation may be more equitable in terms of the manner in which tax burdens are distributed among different income groups. On balance, the overall tax rate structure of New York tends to be slightly progressive; that of Washington is highly regressive; the California tax rate structure tends toward proportionality, although it may be regressive at family income levels below $2,500. Insofar as social value criteria are concerned, the Washington tax structure is highly inequitable; New York's is consistent with the ability-to-pay principle of taxation; the California system plots a more or less middle course. The question of tax burden distribution in California will be analyzed in detail in Chapter 5.[10]

[10] For an excellent summary comparison of the California tax structure with that of a selected group of other states, see the Report of the Senate Fact Finding Committee on Revenue and Taxation, *Comparison of the Tax Structure of California with Selected other States, 1952 to 1963*, Senate of the State of California, January 1965.

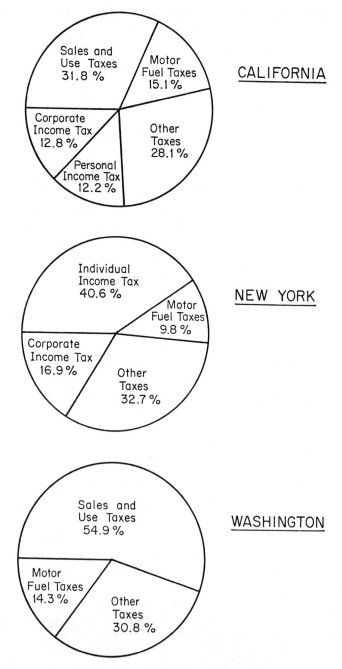

Fig. 7

Table 24. Comparison of California tax structure with New York and Washington 1963
(thousands of dollars)

Type of tax	California		New York		Washington	
	Total revenue	% of total taxes	Total revenue	% of total taxes	Total revenue	% of total taxes
Sales and use	$ 813,310	31.8	—	—	$301,735	54.9
Individual income	321,921	12.8	1,018,704	40.6	—	—
Corporation net income	311,275	12.2	423,243	16.9	—	—
Motor fuels	386,671	15.1	244,768	9.8	78,382	14.3
Death and gift	92,248	3.6	91,299	3.6	14,160	2.6
Other	633,858	24.5	728,770	29.1	155,409	28.2
Total taxes	$2,559,283	100.0	$2,506,784	100.0	$549,686	100.0

Source: U.S. Department of Commerce, Bureau of the Census, Compendium of State Government Finances.

State general fund expenditures in California

In the five-year interval from 1960 to 1965, personal income in California increased at an annual average rate of $3.3 billion. State

Table 25. General fund expenditure in California 1965

	Amount	Percent of total expenditures
State operations		
Legislative.....................................$	3,485,631	0.2
Judicial......................................	3,765,754	0.2
Executive (excluding state disaster office)..........	2,471,003	0.1
General administration.........................	11,659,512	0.5
Agriculture...................................	11,657,294	0.5
Corrections...................................	96,314,446	4.2
Education....................................	13,761,744	0.6
Higher education.............................	120,646,419	5.2
University of California........................	171,496,724	7.4
Fiscal affairs................................	39,176,006	1.7
Health and welfare............................	191,229,031	8.3
Highway transportation........................	217,082	——
Industrial relations............................	21,555,532	0.9
Justice......................................	11,003,303	0.5
Military affairs...............................	3,274,288	0.1
Regulation and licensing.......................	16,542,344	0.7
Resources...................................	53,982,042	2.4
Veterans affairs..............................	7,244,967	0.3
Miscellaneous................................	1,101,057	0.1
Debt service (excluding state school building bonds)............................	30,517,219	1.3
Total state operations.......................$	811,101,398	35.2
Capital outlay		
Total expenditures for capital outlay.............$	28,670,929	1.2
Local assistance		
Corrections...................................$	3,417,932	0.2
Education....................................	1,013,383,422	43.9
Health and welfare...........................	424,070,123	18.4
Resources...................................	18,440,141	0.8
For other purposes............................	7,464,248	0.3
Total local assistance...................$1,466,775,866 (See detail on page 53)		63.6
Total general fund governmental cost expenditures........................$2,306,548,193		100.0

Source: State Controller, *Annual Report.*

Table 26. General fund expenditure for local assistance in California 1965

Local assistance expenditures	Amount	* Percent of total expenditures
Corrections		
Juvenile homes and camps...................$	3,417,932	0.2
Education		
Public schools.............................$	894,264,254**	38.8
State school building aid—debt service........	45,411,436	2.0
Free textbooks...........................	13,487,812	0.6
Contributions to teachers' retirement system.....	52,513,029	2.2
Other....................................	7,706,891	0.3
Total education.....................$1,013,383,422		43.9
Health and welfare		
Mental hygiene		
Establish and maintain mental health services..............................$	10,522,302	0.5
Public health		
Administration of local agencies............$	4,828,963	0.2
Maintenance of tuberculosis sanitoria........	3,297,199	0.1
Services for physically handicapped children..............................	10,439,879	0.5
Construction of hospital facilities............	11,644,070	0.5
Other public health purposes...............	275,530	—
Total public health...................$	30,485,641	1.3
Social welfare		
Old age security..........................$	199,808,402	8.7
Aid to blind.............................	10,959,212	0.5
Aid to families with dependent children......	118,186,012	5.1
Aid to disabled..........................	46,756,418	2.0
Other social welfare purposes..............	7,352,136	0.3
Total social welfare..................$	383,062,180	16.6
Total health and welfare.............$	424,070,123	18.4
Resources		
Natural resources.........................$	88,968	—
Water resources..........................	18,351,173	0.8
Total resources......................$	18,440,141	0.8
For other purposes		
Salaries of superior court judges.............$	5,406,198	0.2
Miscellaneous other purposes................	2,058,050	0.1
Total other purposes..................$	7,464,248	0.3
Total local assistance.................$1,466,775,866		63.6

* Computed as a percentage of total governmental cost expenditures.
** In addition $40,290,677 was transferred from the California Water Fund to the State School Fund for this purpose during the 1964–1965 fiscal year and $34,365,298 was transferred in the 1963–1964 fiscal year.

general fund expenditures during the same period increased at an average rate of $173.2 million each year. Roughly speaking, Californians were investing about 5.0 cents of each dollar increment of personal income in general fund expenditures in the first half of the decade of the 1960's. Expenditures increased from $1.6 billion in 1960 to $2.3 billion in 1965. Here is further empirical evidence of the costs of urban growth and industrialization.

General fund expenditures in California cover state operations, minor capital outlays, and assistance to local government. It is particularly significant to note that 63.6 percent of the expenditures in 1965 were dedicated to assist local governments in the areas of corrections, education, health and welfare, and resource development. This indicates that the fiscal system of local government in California is inextricably bound to the state's revenue structure. It indicates, moreover, the general limitations of the local tax system, particularly the property tax.

Of the $1.46 billion allocated to local assistance, $1.0 billion, 43.9 percent, was channeled into the public education program to underwrite school district current operating expenses, debt service on state school building aid bonds, textbooks, the Teachers' Retirement System and other miscellaneous costs of public education. The equivalent of all state general fund revenue produced by the retail sales and use tax ($939.3 million), bank and corporation franchise and income taxes ($416.4 million) and the cigarette tax ($74.5 million) is committed by constitutional or statutory provisions to assist local government. These facts deny the myth of local fiscal autonomy in California.

The analysis of this chapter has revealed that state finance in California is greatly dependent upon the federal grant-in-aid program; local government, in turn, is receiving considerable financial assistance from the state. There is no implication that these intergovernmental fiscal relationships are bad; they merely provide the background against which future changes in the state-local revenue system must be considered. In this, the urban-industrial age, it appears that federal-state-local fiscal relationships are intertwined. Issues in taxation and public policy recommendations must, accordingly, be considered within this framework. One thing is certain: The era of fiscal isolation has clearly ended.

A policy framework for a modern state-local system of taxation

> Civilized countries mold their people into civilized ways of thinking, guided by values that experience and knowledge have laid down. We don't leave it to the market. We educate. Only in this way can we achieve the great goals of a civilized society. —*Alvin H. Hansen*

In the first chapter it was suggested that an adequate state-local system of taxation is a prerequisite for the realization of orderly community and economic growth. In subsequent chapters the salient facts, problem areas, and public policy implications of state and local finance in California were outlined. Local units of government continue to rely heavily upon the property tax; the state revenue system is heavily oriented toward consumer-spending taxes. The fiscal problems of local government, and the policy implications of local finance emerge as priority areas for legislative action. Sustained population and economic growth indicate that both state and local units of government in California must find new sources of revenue.

There are, then, two primary concerns: First, to improve the revenue system, particularly in the matter of eliminating existing inequities; second, to enhance the revenue-generating capacity of the state-local system of taxation.

The political process provides the mechanism with which to work out fiscal problems. Ideally, the political process should operate within a well-defined public policy framework which reflects the philosophy, values, and goals of the greater society. When public policy is not based upon social needs, the political arena becomes a breeding ground of social injustice. Existing state and local tax systems, the latter in particular, are indicative of an historical gap between the ideal and the real in the public policy framework governing developments in taxation.

In this chapter the attributes of a policy framework which provides a bridge between the state-local tax system as it *is* and the tax system as it *ought* to be are outlined in terms of the generally accepted principles and criteria that should govern a system of public finance in a democratic society. Those who formally work within the political process might very well reflect on this framework, which may bring into focus guidelines for state-local taxation policy other than those defined by political expediency.

The benefit principle of taxation

California's system of freeways and roads is financed under the benefit principle of taxation which holds that the beneficiary of a government spending program should bear the cost. Most students of taxation would agree that the benefits-received principle should be applied as an integral part of a modern system of public finance. To the extent that the citizen's tax payment is linked directly to an expenditure program from which he benefits, greater awareness of the positive role of government is achieved.

What logical constraints should govern the application of the benefit principle? Five may be identified, and it is suggested that all must be present if the principle is to be applied in a manner consistent with generally accepted criteria. First, it should be possible to trace directly the benefits received from the government program to the economic unit concerned. Defense expenditures, for example, obviously do not meet this condition. Second, the money value of the government good or service should be measurable; that is, it should be possible to assign a price[1] to that which is received. Regional recreation, waste disposal, special services and privileges can all be valued in money terms, establishing a basis for distributing tax responsibilities. Third, the benefit principle has applicability when the per unit tax (or price) is relatively small. This assures most, if not all, citizens access to the government

[1] Price is simply the economic value of the good or service measured in terms of money.

program, at the same time allowing the realization of economies of scale in the production of the good or service.

Fourth, the application of the pure benefit principle of taxation assumes that the economic ability to bear the cost of the service exists. By way of illustration, it would be a contradiction in terms to argue that the Aid to Needy Children Program should be financed according to the benefits received. Fifth, an effective program of taxation under the benefit principle depends upon the administrative feasibility of the program. If the economic costs of collection and administration exceed the revenues received, no strong case can be made for financing a governmental program on this basis.

Local units of government, in particular, should plan to extend the benefit principle to the financing of appropriate functions where these five conditions are met. Certainly the fee structure governing the allocations of water under the California Water Plan should give recognition to the economic benefits received by the users of the water. One of the leading issues concerns the price structure applicable to urban, industrial, and agricultural users of the water. Cost/benefit relationships should, in the final analysis, govern this structure.

The ability-to-pay principle of taxation

Simply stated, this concept of taxation is built on the premise that those possessing the economic capacity to do so should pay for the costs of a government program. Application of the principle involves two ever-present questions: "How shall we measure the ability to pay taxes?" and "How rapidly does the ability to bear taxes increase as the tax base increases?" These questions have often carried the implication that there is no feasible basis upon which to apply the ability principle.

With respect to the first question, a society has at least three explicit, measurable bases for determining the ability to pay taxes. These are: income, wealth, and spending. One might even add a fourth basis for taxation—saving. This, however, would violate one of the magnificent myths governing modern fiscal policy. The classical line of reasoning argues that we must not dry up the fountains of saving that flow automatically into real investment in capital goods. This analysis has little validity in the modern corporate society where separation of ownership and control exists, and where internal sources of financing underwrite the largest share of new investment. Under existing fiscal policy, however, the tax base may be correlated with income, wealth, or spending—not saving. The choice, or combination of choices, will be conditioned by social value attitudes toward thrift, spending, wealth accumulation, individualism, etc. All three bases are used in the California state-local system of finance.

The question of how rapidly one's ability to pay taxes increases as his income, wealth, or spending increases is more difficult to answer. Some would argue that proportionality, that is, the same percentage tax rate over the entire range of the tax base, measures the ability to pay; others, on the other hand, hold that the tax rate should increase as the base, e.g., income, increases.

Obviously these two concepts of ability are irreconcilable. They each rest on premises that are largely assertive in nature. The premises, in turn, are built upon alternative assumptions concerning the marginal utility, or satisfaction, derived from increments of income, wealth, or spending.

In other words, one set of premises leads logically to a concept of proportionality in defining the appropriate relationship between the tax base and the tax rate; another set of premises leads to progressivity in the rate structure. Both are largely products of their respective economic philosophies. Whether one favors proportionality or progressivity, or even regressivity, as a measure of the ability to pay taxes depends in the main on one's social value structure and ideas of individual utility function. The latter establishes the schedule of relationships between money income and the utility derived from that income.

Whatever the direction of the formal academic dialogue or the philosophical debate, the social consensus in the United States for several decades has supported the concept of progressivity in personal income taxation as conforming with the ability principle. This concept states that the ability to bear taxes increases both absolutely and relatively with increases in income.

The social acceptability of the ability principle may be enhanced by linking it to the expenditure side of the governmental process, which is the same procedure used in establishing a rationale for the benefit principle of taxation. This means that the ability-to-pay principle of taxation should be applied when the benefits from an expenditure program will be broadly diffused throughout the society. Here a second essential dimension of the ability principle in its applicability to modern fiscal affairs can be identified. It has already been indicated that ability is consistent with progressivity in the tax rate structure as such. Now it is suggested that progressively inclined tax rate structures be utilized in financing defense, education, research and development, programs of protection, etc., where the benefits are widely distributed throughout the society, and where the general criteria guiding the application of the benefit principle are not met. On the tax extraction side, ability denotes progressivity; on the expenditure side, wide diffusion of benefits appears to be most compatible with the ability principle.

The position that such government functions as defense, public education, and law enforcement should be financed under the ability principle is based on logic. In every instance, the benefits are broadly diffused throughout the society, accruing to those possessing life, enjoying liberty, and pursuing happiness. The relationship between progressivity in the tax extraction process and broadly diffused benefits on the expenditure side is the epitome of fiscal equity. Unfortunately, few state and local tax systems measure up to this concept of fiscal equity.

Public education, by way of example, produces social, economic, cultural, and personal benefits which extend far beyond the individual involved in the process. Yet, in California a large portion of the costs of public education is financed with a property tax demonstrated to be highly inequitable in its pattern of burden distribution. In effect, education, which produces widely diffused benefits to the society, is financed on the "inability-to-pay" principle of taxation. This is one of the major contradictions of the California fiscal system.

This is merely one illustration of the many inconsistencies in contemporary state and local public finance policies. We commit ourselves to a highly commendable social policy on the expenditure side, i.e., equal opportunity for a high-quality education at public expense; yet we vitiate the net social gain by heavy reliance on regressive property and sales taxes at the state and local levels of government. These contradictions are placed side by side because they illustrate the priority need for the articulation and implementation of a new public policy framework within which to meet the fiscal responsibilities of the next several decades. The remedy rests in a comprehensive reform of the state-local system of taxation through the legislative process.

The criteria of a socially acceptable tax system

The benefit and ability principles represent the general public policy guidelines that should govern the development of a system of taxation. There are, in addition, certain criteria that a tax system should meet. From the total range of social priorities, here are four of the most important broad criteria, illustrated by way of a set of maxims of modern taxation: *Maxim 1*—The tax system should be compatible with the social value criteria which govern the general social processes. For example, if the society believes in social justice, the tax system should distribute its burdens in equitable fashion. *Maxim 2*—The revenue system should be fiscally adequate, broadly based, stable in its yield, and balanced in its final incidence. These are the fiscal criteria of an ideal tax system. *Maxim 3*—The tax system should be administratively simple, economical to administer, with clearly defined tax bases and tax rate structures. *Maxim 4*—Taxes should have minimum adverse affects on economic productivity, resource allocation, and the levels of employment, income and output.

There is, then, an explicit set of *social value, fiscal, administrative,* and *economic* criteria that should govern state-local tax programs in California. Each has its place and should assume an appropriate value in the formula of modern taxation.

However, in the arena of practical affairs where issues of taxation are finally decided, we rarely find a balanced application of these criteria. The college professor may preoccupy himself with the issue of equity in taxation; the businessman may be concerned with only the economic effects on incentives, productivity, etc; the elected official and program administrator may stress the administrative aspects of the taxation process; because most, if not all of us, are against taxation, per se, the all-important matter of fiscal adequacy receives little attention.

Each individual or interest group argues for the particular criterion which best protects its own area of interest or concern. Yet, in the final analysis, a socially tolerable system of taxation must incorporate and sustain a delicate balance of the social value, fiscal, administrative, and economic criteria. There are no valid ethical absolutes governing the priority assigned to each of these criteria in a revenue system. No tax system can be absolutely equitable, nor can it avoid some adverse economic effects. A concept of ethical relativism should govern the revenue system. It is desirable to achieve minimums of inequity, administrative complexity, and adverse economic effects. The dynamics of the social process may change the relative importance attached to each criterion, but those who command the legislative process and others engaged in the dialogue should give due recognition to all four of them.

To the extent that the existing system of revenue distributes its burdens inequitably, is administratively complex, and uneconomic in its effects, an appropriate program of tax reform must be initiated without delay. The program of reform should be consistent with the benefit and ability principles and within the context of the social value, fiscal, administrative, and economic criteria. These principles and criteria are the essence of the policy framework. Insofar as the fiscal capabilities of the existing revenue system need to be bolstered to meet increased expenditures, again these principles and criteria should govern. Historically, most programs of tax reform have been piecemeal in nature, failing to grapple with the major social value, fiscal, administrative, and economic shortcomings of the revenue system. However, because more facts are becoming available on the manner in which tax burdens are distributed, and because the forces of urbanization will require additional state and local taxes, the time for tax reform is propitious. It is essential that programs of tax reform and revision be guided by these generally accepted social principles and criteria. Political expediency alone provides a socially unacceptable criterion or rationale from which to evolve modern taxation policies.

The distribution of tax burdens in California

Democracies can not afford
To let injustice be ignored,
Though it might cause them some surprise
To find just where injustice lies.
We know less clearly what is meant
By Justice than by Discontent,
And so the search for Justice leads
To balancing Dessert with Needs.
                —*Kenneth E. Boulding*

5

The issue of how tax burdens are distributed within the private sector of the society is the most prominent question in public finance today. Very little empirical evidence is available indicating precisely how tax burdens are distributed among business and household units. Students of public finance have been content to deal in generalities so far as the question of tax burdens is concerned. Yet, before intelligent tax reform and revision can be effected, it is essential to develop definitive data on this complex question. By proceeding without such information the probabilities of compounding existing injustices are very high.

Having elaborated upon the public policy framework that should guide future tax legislation in California, the next logical step in the program of reform involves a factual analysis of the manner in which state-local taxes are borne. The factual picture must be placed within the context of the policy framework in order that the *real* and the *ideal* may be compared. The legislative process must narrow the gap between the two.

There are no automatic forces within the social organism that will bring the realities of the taxation process into an ideal state. On the contrary, the inherent forces at work will tend to widen the gap between the tax system as it is and the tax system as it ought to be. We would expect a pragmatically-oriented society to resist persuasive arguments based on ideology; we are wagering that people will be more effectively made aware of the deficiencies of the existing state-local tax system in California by being exposed to the factual realities of the pattern of tax burden distribution. Such is the goal of the present chapter.

Comparative state-local tax and expenditure burdens

In the period from 1940 to 1965, California's population increased by 12 million persons; total personal income increased from $5.8 billion to $60.0 billion; per capita personal income rose from $840 to $3,100; over one million new jobs were created in manufacturing lines of activity. These economic indicators provide a measure of the magnitude of the unprecedented urbanization and economic forces operating within the California economy during the past 25 years. Since population and economic growth create demands for new public goods and services, these facts are essential background for a discussion of comparative tax burdens.

As revealed in Table 27, California, the most populous and fastest-growing state, ranked second behind Alaska in state-local per capita general expenditures in 1964. California state and local units of government expended $417.93 per capita (excluding federal grants) as compared with the national average of $299.25. California's ranking on a comparative basis is consistent with the high rate of urban and economic growth. Moreover, the ranking is consistent with the general high quality of the education system, freeway system, standards of protection, law enforcement, and government in the state. The citizen receives in public goods and services pretty much what he is willing to pay for. The public sector is comparable with the private sector in this respect.

Are Californians over-burdened with state-local tax responsibilities in comparison with citizens of other states? The answer is no! In terms of general revenue of state-local governments collected per $1,000 of personal income, the figure for 1963 was $129.32. This placed California 20th among the states. If the average of all 50 states, $117.61, is equated to an "effort index" of 100, California scored 110 on the scale for relative effort in producing state-local general revenue per $1,000 of personal income in 1963. Mississippi, with collections of $138.58 and an effort index rating of 119, ranked well above California. This would indicate that in the relative sense Californians are not bearing an oppressive state-local tax burden. The results are particularly surprising in view of California's rapid growth. The data may indicate that state and local units in California are producing a large volume of high quality services for each dollar of general revenue extracted from the private sector. The state-local tax dollar may be spent more efficiently than most citizens are willing to admit.

Table 27. State-local per capita general expenditure with and without federal grants, all states, 1963

State	Expenditure including federal grants	Amount of federal grants	Expenditure less federal grants		
			Net expenditure	Rank	Expenditure relative
United States..........$343.64	$ 44.39	$299.25	—	100
Alaska................ 670.10	176.56	493.54	(1)	165
California............. 464.98	47.05	417.93	(2)	139
Hawaii................ 460.30	49.41	410.89	(3)	137
Nevada............... 491.97	84.40	407.57	(4)	136
New York............. 432.84	34.62	398.22	(5)	133
Washington........... 430.98	53.60	377.38	(6)	126
Wyoming............. 506.68	145.10	361.58	(7)	121
Wisconsin............. 385.78	34.06	351.72	(8)	118
Oregon............... 403.96	60.61	343.35	(9)	114
Colorado............. 401.44	63.28	338.16	(10)	113
Minnesota............ 374.72	43.20	331.52	(11)	111
Michigan............. 366.86	36.91	329.95	(12)	110
Delaware............. 386.09	58.41	327.68	(13)	109
Connecticut........... 364.19	37.09	327.10	(14)	109
North Dakota......... 382.69	60.85	321.84	(15)	107
Massachusetts......... 359.15	39.67	319.48	(16)	106
Utah................. 380.95	67.84	313.11	(17)	104
Arizona.............. 372.79	59.73	313.06	(18)	104
Montana............. 399.97	90.31	309.66	(19)	103
Kansas............... 345.72	39.40	306.32	(20)	102
Iowa................. 341.16	36.82	304.34	(21)	101
New Mexico.......... 381.37	79.40	301.97	(22)	100
Maryland............ 332.47	36.68	295.79	(23)	99
Florida.............. 322.50	33.00	289.50	(24)	97
Vermont............. 366.57	78.93	287.64	(25)	96

Table 27. State-local per capita general expenditure with and without federal grants, all states, 1963 (continued)

State	Expenditure including federal grants	Amount of federal grants	Expenditure less federal grants		
			Net expenditure	Rank	Expenditure relative
Illinois................	323.71	38.23	285.48	(26)	95
South Dakota..........	348.75	64.07	284.68	(27)	95
New Jersey............	310.64	27.92	282.72	(28)	94
Louisiana..............	356.80	74.58	282.22	(29)	94
New Hampshire........	322.58	45.76	276.82	(30)	92
Pennsylvania..........	308.16	37.14	271.02	(31)	90
Idaho.................	342.12	72.78	269.34	(32)	90
Oklahoma.............	345.48	76.27	269.21	(33)	90
Rhode Island..........	315.66	47.51	268.15	(34)	89
Indiana...............	298.51	30.67	267.84	(35)	89
Nebraska.............	312.92	48.54	264.38	(36)	88
Ohio.................	299.98	37.21	262.77	(37)	88
Maine................	302.47	51.49	250.98	(38)	83
Missouri..............	294.69	49.95	244.74	(39)	82
Kentucky.............	294.54	55.64	238.90	(40)	80
Texas................	282.46	43.80	238.66	(41)	80
Virginia...............	275.89	42.59	233.30	(42)	78
Georgia..............	276.31	50.48	225.83	(43)	75
Tennessee............	255.85	56.68	199.17	(44)	67
North Carolina........	232.33	35.45	196.88	(45)	66
West Virginia..........	250.72	54.58	196.14	(46)	65
Mississippi............	252.66	59.19	193.47	(47)	64
Alabama..............	248.07	55.03	193.04	(48)	64
Arkansas.............	242.82	65.96	176.86	(49)	59
South Carolina........	210.44	37.10	173.34	(50)	58

Sources: *Governmental Finances in 1963*, p. 45; *Social Security Bulletin* (June 1964), p. 21.

Californians paid over $9.0 billion in federal taxes in 1962. The per capita incidence of federal taxes in the United States in that year was $512; the comparable figure for California was $642, placing the state in sixth place behind Delaware, Connecticut, New York, Nevada, and New Jersey. California is a relatively prosperous and wealthy state. It is not surprising to find per capita federal taxes above the national average. A large share of these funds is returned to the state economy under a

Table 28. General revenue of state-local governments collected from own sources per $1,000 of personal income, all states, 1963

State	General revenue per $1,000 of income	Effort relative
United States..........................	$117.61	100
New Mexico..........................	154.77	132
North Dakota........................	153.68	131
Louisiana............................	153.14	130
Wyoming............................	145.09	123
Minnesota...........................	142.31	121
Wisconsin............................	141.08	120
South Dakota........................	140.94	120
Arizona..............................	140.58	120
Mississippi..........................	138.58	119
Alaska...............................	137.68	118
Washington..........................	135.42	115
Montana.............................	134.90	115
Kansas...............................	134.88	115
Hawaii...............................	134.03	114
Colorado............................	133.75	114
Vermont.............................	131.41	112
Idaho................................	130.52	111
New York............................	130.07	111
Iowa.................................	129.85	110
California............................	129.32	110
Oklahoma............................	128.03	109
Oregon..............................	125.87	107
Utah.................................	125.74	107
Michigan.............................	124.81	106
Florida...............................	122.56	104
Nevada..............................	119.58	102
Maine................................	118.22	101
Texas................................	117.86	100
West Virginia........................	116.20	99
Arkansas.............................	115.70	98
Georgia..............................	115.38	98
South Carolina.......................	114.07	97
North Carolina.......................	113.73	97
Kentucky.............................	111.56	95
Alabama.............................	111.47	95
Nebraska.............................	110.75	94

State	General revenue per $1,000 of income	Effort relative
Massachusetts	110.00	94
Rhode Island	108.94	93
Tennessee	108.94	93
Indiana	107.52	91
New Hampshire	107.31	91
Maryland	102.36	87
Ohio	102.21	87
Pennsylvania	101.54	86
New Jersey	99.99	85
Connecticut	99.63	85
Illinois	99.33	85
Virginia	99.05	84
Delaware	97.80	83
Missouri	93.84	80

Source: *Governmental Finances in 1963*, p. 50.

variety of federal grant and expenditure programs. Californians do not fare badly in the arena of federal finance. When combined per capita federal and state-local general revenues are compared, the Californian pays at least $100 less in taxes than the New Yorker.

State-local expenditures in relation to state personal income

The internal consistency of the preceding analysis is borne out by relating total state-local expenditures (current operating *plus* capital outlays) to total state personal income since 1930. It is surprising to find that, despite the rapid population and economic growth during the past 25 years, the percentage of state-local spending in relation to personal income is no higher in the 1960's than during the depression decade of the 1930's. See Figure 8.

In 1933, for example, 15.4 cents out of each dollar of personal income was impounded to finance state-local expenditures. In 1965,

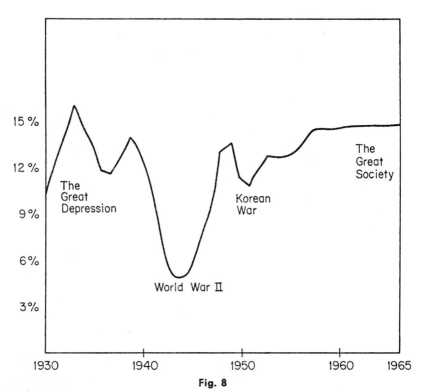

Fig. 8

state-local spending in California reached an estimated level of $8.1 billion; personal income reached $60.0 billion. In the mid-1960's, Californians were allocating 13.5 cents out of each dollar of expanding personal income to finance state and local spending. The data in Table

Table 29. Total tax collections in California 1950–1951, 1960–1961, 1963–1964 (billions of dollars)

	1950–51	1960–61	1963–64
Federal	$3.731	$ 8.486	$10.535
State	.943	2.490	3.369
Local	.862	2.522	3.222
Total taxes	$5.536	$13.498	$17.126
Total taxes as a percentage of state personal income	26.1%	30.4%	31.5%

Source: California State Board of Equalization, *Annual Report 1963–1964*, p. 3.

Table 30. Estimated per capita incidence of federal taxes, all states, 1962

State	Tax incidence	Ratio of tax incidence to average incidence
United States....................	$ 516	1.00
Delaware.......................	$1,072	2.08
Connecticut.....................	801	1.55
New York.......................	750	1.45
Nevada........................	662	1.28
New Jersey	648	1.26
California......................	642	1.24
Illinois.........................	637	1.23
Massachusetts...................	636	1.23
Maryland.......................	574	1.11
Pennsylvania....................	569	1.10
Rhode Island....................	566	1.10
Ohio...........................	548	1.06
Michigan.......................	530	1.03
Colorado.......................	514	.99
Washington.....................	513	.99
Wyoming.......................	503	.97
New Hampshire..................	501	.97
Oregon........................	498	.97
Missouri	491	.95
Hawaii.........................	489	.95
Wisconsin......................	486	.94
Indiana........................	458	.89
Florida........................	455	.88
Minnesota......................	446	.86
Alaska.........................	444	.86
Nebraska.......................	428	.83
Arizona........................	421	.82
Maine.........................	418	.81
Montana.......................	415	.80
Kansas........................	413	.80
Texas.........................	410	.79
Vermont.......................	405	.78
Virginia.......................	395	.77
Iowa..........................	390	.76
Utah..........................	381	.74
Oklahoma......................	376	.73
Idaho.........................	358	.69
New Mexico....................	355	.69
Louisiana......................	349	.68
West Virginia...................	346	.67

Table 30. Estimated per capita incidence of federal taxes, all states, 1962 (continued)

State	Tax incidence	Ratio of tax incidence to average incidence
Kentucky........................	316	.61
Georgia.........................	315	.61
Tennessee.......................	311	.60
North Dakota....................	309	.60
South Dakota....................	301	.58
North Carolina..................	296	.57
Alabama........................	277	.54
South Carolina..................	255	.49
Arkansas........................	236	.46
Mississippi......................	196	.37

Source: Tax Foundation, *Facts and Figures on Government Finance* (1963), p. 112.

31 indicate that California's real economic growth is underwriting the costs of urbanization and industrialization, with no significant encroachment on the private sector's historical share of disposable income. Moderate encroachments on business and personal income may be necessary if the desired social balance between private and public goods is to be achieved during the next decade. Current economic growth rates, measured in terms of expanding personal income, employment, and gross state product, suggest that the socially necessary increases in absolute and relative state-local tax burdens can be assumed without undue sacrifices in the private sector as a whole. The important issue concerns the manner in which the increased tax burdens are distributed between the business and household sectors, and among income groups within the private sector.[1]

Distribution of direct state-local tax burdens in California between the business and household sectors

How are the direct burdens of state and local public finance distributed between the household and business sectors in California? This

[1] For an excellent detailed analysis of state and local expenditure patterns in California, see *California Local Finance, op. cit.*, pp. 67–134.

Table 31. Comparison of personal income to combined state and local government expenditures, California, 1930–1965

Year	(Millions) Personal income	(Millions) Total state-local gov't expenditures	Total expenditures as percent of personal income
1930................$	5,079	$ 491.6	9.68%
1931................	4,347	505.6	11.63
1932................	3,381	498.0	14.73
1933................	3,227	497.1	15.40
1934................	3,590	512.0	14.26
1935................	4,020	533.5	13.27
1936................	4,817	543.8	11.29
1937................	5,132	565.8	11.02
1938................	5,088	620.9	12.20
1939................	5,257	714.5	13.59
1940................	5,839	731.1	12.52
1941................	7,331	744.4	10.15
1942................	10,010	723.3	7.23
1943................	13,281	679.1	5.11
1944................	14,653	692.1	4.72
1945................	15,194	741.8	4.88
1946................	16,084	1,007.1	6.26
1947................	16,637	1,226.7	7.37
1948................	17,610	1,651.2	9.38
1949................	17,835	2,244.3	12.58
1950................	19,627	2,572.7	13.10
1951................	22,726	2,457.3	10.81
1952................	25,089	2,646.6	10.55
1953................	26,642	2,970.7	11.15
1954................	27,483	3,381.8	12.31
1955................	30,224	3,670.0	12.14
1956................	33,273	4,078.0	12.26
1957................	35,582	4,458.0	12.53
1958................	37,241	5,016.0	13.47
1959................	40,960	5,715.0	13.95
1960................	43,122	6,021.0	13.96
1961*................	45,586	6,360.0	13.95
1962*................	47,250	6,600.0	13.97
1965*................	60,000	8,100.0	13.50

* Estimated

Sources: Personal income data from *California Statistical Abstract*. Expenditure data, 1930–1955, from *Tax Digest,* March 1956, p. 78. Expenditure data, 1956–1960, compiled from *U.S. Statistical Abstract* tables on state and local expenditures for individual years. Data for 1961, 1962 and 1965 estimated by the author.

question can be placed into a factual perspective by examining the sources of the $6.5 billion in general revenues raised by state and local units of government in fiscal year 1963. The analysis here is concerned with the point of legal impact of the tax burden; the burden implications of tax shifting will be treated separately.

The $4.0 billion in locally-generated revenues in 1963 were provided by property taxes (67.5%), fees and charges (12.5%), sales taxes (7.5%), and other revenues (12.5%). The data in Table 32 reveal that between 60 and 65 percent of the initial property tax burden in California rests upon the household sector. In the case of the sales tax, 100 percent of the impact (and incidence) is on the consumer. If we assume that the impact of 75 percent of local fees and charges and 66.6 percent of miscellaneous revenues and taxes rests on consumers, approximately 70 percent of the initial local revenue burden in California is placed upon household units. If recognition is given to the possibility of shifting certain taxes by business in the short-run, household units bear at least 80 percent of the ultimate local revenue burden in California. Therefore, of the $4.0 billion raised locally in 1963, it is reasonable to assume that $3.2 billion ultimately was borne by the household sector. As a rule-of-thumb for public policy decision-making, it is reasonable to assume that 80 percent of the local tax burden in the short-run rests on households; 20 percent of the ultimate burden, or incidence, falls on the business sector. See Figures 9 and 10.

State general fund and motor vehicle revenues in 1963 amounted to $2.5 billion. Household units assumed the initial impact of 70.0 percent of this revenue burden. The percentage contribution to total state revenues by household units from various tax sources was as follows:

Sales and use tax	30.5%
Personal income	13.0
Alcoholic beverages	2.7
Horse racing	1.7
Cigarettes	2.6
Highway user	15.0*
Vehicle in lieu taxes	4.4**
Percent of total state revenue	69.9%

* Represents 75 percent of total; 25 percent allocated to business sector.
** Represents 80 percent of total yield to state.

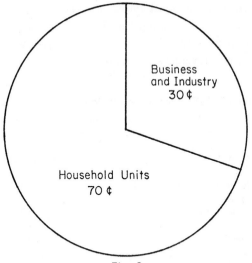

Fig. 9

Householders bore the legal impact of $1.75 billion in state taxes during 1963. Once again, if recognition is given to the fact that certain lines of business and industrial activity can shift taxes forward to consumers in the short-run, it is not unreasonable to assume for public policy purposes that household units in California bear at least 80.0 percent of the

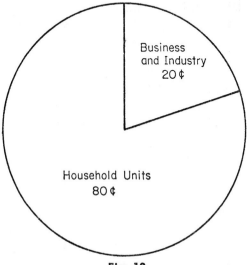

Fig. 10

state tax burden. Both the local and state revenue systems place a large proportion of the initial legal burden (impact) and the final economic burden (incidence) on household units. These facts must be taken into consideration as new revenue sources are sought.

Table 32. Estimated property tax paid by class of property in California 1961

Class of property	Percentage of assessed value*
Single family homes	41.7
Other residential	5.6
Farms and acreage	6.0
Vacant lots	2.3
Commercial	10.8
Other	3.5
Public utility	11.0
Personal property	14.6
Industrial	4.9

* Figures may not add to 100 due to rounding.
Source: Assembly Interim Committee on Revenue and Taxation, *Taxation of Property in California,* Vol. 4, No. 12, December 1964, p. 27.

Distribution of property, retail sales, and personal income tax burdens by income groups in California

It will be useful here to review the salient facts of state-local finance in California. First, at least 70.0 percent of the legal impact of the total tax burden falls on household units. Second, at least 45.0 percent of local revenues and 88.0 percent of locally-levied taxes are produced by the property tax. Third, at least 60.0 percent of the initial impact of the property tax rests on household units. Fourth, the 3.0 percent state sales and use tax yields over 40.0 percent of all general fund revenues. Fifth, the major burden of the state-local tax system in California falls on the consumption spending of householders.

The all-important public policy question, then, becomes that of determining how state-local tax burdens are distributed among different income groups within the household sector. An empirical analysis of the pattern of burden distribution of property, retail sales, and personal income taxes in California is presented at this point. These are the major taxes impinging upon household units. The results of this analysis will graphically demonstrate the gross inequities of the property tax. The factual findings, moreover, will take the question of inequity in property taxation out of the realm of philosophical speculation and demonstrate why local units of government must find new sources of revenue to finance future needs.

DISTRIBUTION OF PROPERTY TAX BURDENS IN CALIFORNIA. The data in Table 33 summarize the manner in which local property tax burdens were distributed in California during the period 1960–1962.[2]

Table 33. Distribution of property tax burdens in California 1960–1962

Family income level*	Average effective tax rate	Average dollar tax burden
$ 2,000	9.0%**	$180
3,000	8.5**	255
4,000	7.2	288
5,000	5.3	265
6,000	4.1	246
7,000	3.9	273
8,000	3.7	296
9,000	3.4	306
10,000	3.1	310
12,000	3.2	384
14,000	3.1	434
16,000	3.0**	480
18,000	3.0**	540
20,000	3.0**	600

* Defined as adjusted gross income.
** Average effective rates assumed by the author.
Source: Calculated from the Report of Senate Fact Finding Committee on Revenue and Taxation. *Property Taxes and Other Local Revenue Sources,* Senate of the State of California, March 1965, pp. 77 and 78.

[2] The average effective rates from 7.2 to 3.1 percent are based on a sample study of 3,900 owner-occupied properties over a three-year period. The adjusted gross income data for each owner-occupant were derived from his California state income tax return. The sample excluded lower income property owners who did not file income tax returns. Unless otherwise indicated, the effective rates in Table

The schedule of relationships between the effective property tax rate and family income level reveals an exceedingly regressive pattern of distribution. For example, the home owner with $2,000 annual income allocated 9.0 percent, or $180, of his yearly income to property tax payments; the family unit with $10,000 income was committed to pay 3.1 percent of its annual receipts to local government in the form of property taxes. The vagaries of the pattern of burden distribution, particularly in the lower-income groups, should be a matter of serious concern for those who value the criterion of equity in taxation.

Not only is the local property tax in California highly regressive; it actually places a higher absolute dollar tax burden on certain lower segments of family income. As a case in point, it would appear that the family unit with $4,000 annual income pays an average property tax of $288, against $265 for a household with $5,000 annual income. Inasmuch as the former household unit is already living on the other side of affluence, certainly the local tax system should not compound social inequities which already exist.

DISTRIBUTION OF GENERAL FUND CONSUMPTION TAXES IN CALIFORNIA. Total general fund revenues for the state of California amounted to $2.24 billion in fiscal year 1964–1965. Of this total, $1.08 billion, or 48.3 percent, was accounted for by retail sales and use taxes, alcoholic beverage revenues, and the cigarette tax. These magnitudes are indicative of the heavy reliance placed on consumer spendings taxes in California. The retail sales and use tax alone yielded $939.3 million, or 41.9 percent of general fund revenues, in fiscal year 1964–1965.

---

33 were calculated from the set of bracket rates presented in the Report of the Senate Fact Finding Committee on Revenue and Taxation, *Property Taxes and Other Local Revenue Sources,* Senate of the State of California, March 1965, Table 5, p. 77. This excellent study was prepared by Messrs. Max E. Fieser, John G. Ranlett, and William K. Schmelzle. The relationships in Table 33 should be interpreted as averages. As such, they may overstate or understate the actual tax burden of specific households in the sample. For example, there are families in the $2,000 income range who are not bearing a 9 percent property tax burden. The average family at this income level should be living in a dwelling unit with a fair market value of $8,000; the assessed valuation of the home in most California counties would be $2,000. With a $9.00 tax rate, the annual tax liability would be $180. See the author's "Property Tax Payments in Relation to Household Income: A Case Study of Los Angeles County," *National Tax Journal,* June, 1963, pp. 197–199, for roughly comparable findings.

Consumption-based taxes obviously play an important role in California public finance. The important question concerns the manner in which the real income burden of these taxes is distributed over different income groups. Fortunately, as a result of the excellent work of Dr. William H. Hickman, we are able to show, within reasonable limits, the relationship between the effective tax rate and disposable income over various ranges of income. Hickman, in a 1958 study conducted for the state board of equalization, reconstructed the pattern of distribution of the retail sales, use, and other excises levied in California.[3] More recently, he has updated the analysis and developed data which show the pattern of burden distribution for 1960–1961.[4] The results are summarized in Table 34.

Hickman's data and methodology suggest a somewhat irregular overall pattern of burden distribution in the case of California retail sales, use, cigarette and alcoholic beverage excise taxes. These consumer taxes are, however, clearly regressive in the case of the $1,000-to-$2,000 income class in relation to the following segments of family net income: $2,000–$3,000; $4,000–$5,000; $7,500 annual net income and above. The patterns of progressivity between the $2,000–$3,000 and $3,000–$4,000 income brackets, and the $5,000–$6,000 and $6,000–$7,500 levels of income, are related in the main to expenditure patterns and the nature of the tax base.

Although the overall pattern of burden distribution is not regressive, the degree of regressivity that exists in the case of lower income family units vis-à-vis more affluent levels of income should be eliminated by appropriate public policy action in the legislative arena; the regressivity that exists beyond the $6,000–$7,500 income bracket is a matter of lesser social consequence.

The rapidly growing California economy can easily transfer the fiscal burdens currently borne by the lowest income families to other income and economic sectors possessing the demonstrated ability to pay the costs of government. Unfortunately, low income groups are not as actively represented as they should be when new tax measures are

[3] William H. Hickman, "Distribution of the Burden of California Sales and other Excise Taxes," Sacramento: State Board of Equalization, 1958.
[4] Report of the Senate Fact Finding Committee on Revenue and Taxation, *General Fund Consumption Taxes,* Senate of the State of California, January 1965, especially pp. 9–36.

Table 34. Distribution of selected general fund consumption taxes in California 1960–1961

Net income class	Retail sales and use tax		Cigarette tax		Alcoholic beverage		Total burden	
	Absolute	Percent	Absolute	Percent	Absolute	Percent	Absolute	Percent
$ 1,000– 2,000	$ 31.93	1.76	$ 4.02	0.22	$ 1.85	0.10	$ 37.80	2.08
2,000– 3,000	43.62	1.55	6.00	0.21	3.16	0.11	52.78	1.87
3,000– 4,000	70.26	1.84	9.54	0.25	2.94	0.08	82.74	2.17
4,000– 5,000	80.55	1.70	9.96	0.21	5.35	0.11	95.86	2.02
5,000– 6,000	103.42	1.75	12.81	0.22	7.92	0.13	124.15	2.10
6,000– 7,500	143.14	2.00	15.24	0.21	12.13	0.17	170.51	2.38
7,500–10,000	154.82	1.75	15.18	0.17	11.74	0.13	181.74	2.07
10,000–15,000	202.37	1.70	11.10	0.09	18.25	0.15	231.72	1.94
15,000 and over	340.25	1.67	19.14	0.09	28.14	0.14	387.53	1.90

Source: Report of the Senate Fact Finding Committee on Revenue and Taxation, General Fund Consumption Taxes, Senate of the State of California, January 1965, pp. 12, 20, 350.

enacted. In the final analysis, the problem of tax burden distribution is not primarily economic; inequities are generally traceable to the philosophical and political dimensions of fiscal policy.

DISTRIBUTION OF RETAIL SALES AND USE TAX BURDENS. Modern students of taxation have commonly theorized that the retail sales and use tax, with food exempted, tends to distribute its burdens proportionately over various levels of income. Yet, the data summarized in Table 35 suggest that the California retail sales and use tax is regressive over

Table 35. Distribution of retail sales and use tax burdens in California 1960–1961

Family disposable income level	Average effective tax rate	Average dollar burden
$ 2,000	1.70%	$ 34.00
3,000	1.62	48.60
4,000	1.87	74.80
5,000	1.70	85.00
6,000	1.81	108.60
7,000	2.00	140.00
8,000	1.87	149.60
9,000	1.81	162.90
10,000	1.75	175.00
12,000	1.70	204.00
14,000	1.67	233.80
16,000	1.66	265.60
18,000	1.64	295.20
20,000	1.63	326.00

Source: Calculated from the Report of the Senate Fact Finding Committee on Revenue and Taxation, *General Fund Consumption Taxes*, Senate of the State of California, January 1965, pp. 12, 13.

several *socially relevant* segments of family income. When considering the equity implications of the manner in which the real income burden of a tax is distributed, it is not sufficient to argue that the overall pattern is mildly progressive up through the $8,000 level of disposable income and moderately regressive in the upper-income brackets. On the contrary, when related to discrete levels of family disposable income, the retail sales and use tax is in fact regressive between the $2,000-to-$3,000, the $4,000-to-$6,000, and the $7,000-to-$20,000 income groups. By broadly describing the overall pattern of burden distribution in terms of mild regressivity and progressivity over only two segments of the income base, we in effect subsume the significant regressivity which exists between smaller segments of income at the lower end of the income scale. In view of growing pressures for increased sales and use tax rates in California, a strong case can be made for removing the burden on family units with less than $3,000 of disposable income by way of a tax credit or direct refund. Higher-income groups possess the economic capacity to absorb the real income sacrifices currently borne by lower-income families under the present system of consumption taxation in California.

DISTRIBUTION OF PERSONAL INCOME TAX BURDENS. Personal income tax rates for married couples filing a joint return in California range from 1.0 percent on the first $5,000 of taxable income to 7.0 percent on taxable income of $30,000 and above. The data in Table 36

Table 36. Distribution of personal income tax burdens in California 1965

Family income level*	Effective tax rate**	Dollar tax burden**
$ 2,000	—	—
3,000	—	—
4,000	—	—
5,000	—	—
6,000	0.14%	$ 8.50
7,000	0.26	18.50
8,000	0.36	28.50
9,000	0.43	38.50
10,000	0.48	48.00
12,000	0.68	82.00
14,000	0.84	118.00
16,000	0.98	156.00
18,000	1.17	210.00
20,000	1.32	264.00

* Defined as adjusted gross income.
** Calculated for a family of four filing a joint return. Tax tables, which reflect allowable deductions and exemptions, were used to compute the tax in the income range from $2,000 to $9,000. A 10 percent "standard deduction" was assumed for income from $10,000 and above.
Source: State of California, *Revenue and Taxation Code*, sections 17041–17045.

illustrate the precise personal income tax burdens borne by a family unit with four members under the provisions of the present California statute. It is interesting to note that this family unit pays no state income tax until *adjusted gross income* reaches $5,300. The tax liability, calculated with the use of tax tables, amounts to $1.50. It is significant to note, further, that the actual dollar burden of the tax is nominal for all family units with annual income under $10,000.

It is sobering to reflect, moreover, that the California family unit in the disposable income range from $2,000 to $3,000 pays more consumption-based taxes ($52.78) than the $48.00 which the family with $10,000 adjusted gross income pays under the state personal income tax. It is difficult to find a plausible social rationale for distributing tax burdens in this manner, at least if equity considerations have any relevance in the development of modern systems of state taxation.

Further insight into the qualitative nature of the manner in which personal income tax responsibilities are distributed in California can be gained from an analysis of the relative importance of different sources of income in the taxable income base. In 1961, personal income tax revenues were derived from the following income sources in the proportions indicated: Salaries and wages, 53.4 percent; proprietorship gains, 11.4 percent; partnership gains, 7.6 percent; capital gains, 12.2 percent; dividends, 7.5 percent; interest, 3.1 percent; rent gains, 2.6 percent; miscellaneous sources, 2.2 percent.[5]

The composite pattern of property, retail sales, and personal income tax distribution in California

Three of the most important sources of state-local tax revenue borne by household units in California were selected for analysis. The property tax yields over 70 percent of all locally-generated county, city, and school district revenues; retail sales and use and personal income taxes provided exactly two-thirds of state general fund revenue in fiscal 1964–1965. It is now possible to develop a comparative analysis of the manner in which the relative and absolute burdens of these three taxes

[5] Report of the Senate Fact Finding Committee on Revenue and Taxation, *The California Personal Income Tax, op. cit.,* p. 40.

have been distributed among household units in recent years. The composite pattern of burden distribution will also emerge from this analysis. The results are summarized in Tables 37 and 38 and in Figure 11.

Table 37. Relative distribution of composite property, sales-use, and personal income tax burdens in California 1960–1962

| Family income level | Effective tax rates | | | |
	Property	Sales	Personal income	Composite
$ 2,000	9.00%	1.70%	——	10.70%
3,000	8.50	1.62	——	10.12
4,000	7.20	1.87	——	9.07
5,000	5.30	1.70	——	7.00
6,000	4.10	1.81	0.14%	6.05
7,000	3.90	2.00	0.26	6.16
8,000	3.70	1.87	0.36	5.93
9,000	3.40	1.81	0.43	5.64
10,000	3.10	1.75	0.48	5.33
12,000	3.20	1.70	0.68	5.58
14,000	3.10	1.67	0.84	5.61
16,000	3.00	1.66	0.98	5.64
18,000	3.00	1.64	1.17	5.81
20,000	3.00	1.63	1.32	5.95

The composite rate structure of these three taxes is steeply regressive, with one exception ($6,000–$7,000), in the entire range of income from $2,000 to $10,000.[6] In California, the family unit with $2,000 of income must dedicate 10.7 percent of its annual income to property and sales taxes. The family with $10,000 of income, on the other hand,

[6] In interpreting the composite rate structure in Table 37 and Figure 11, the reader should keep in mind that the property and personal income tax relationships are based on adjusted gross income; in the case of the retail sales and use tax, the rate structure is based on disposable income. The difference in base does not vitiate the results for several reasons. First, for lower-income groups, adjusted gross and disposable incomes are equal, or nearly so. Second, the composite schedule does not reflect alcoholic beverage and cigarette excises. Third, the 1.0 percent sales and use tax levied by local units of government is not reflected. The composite rate structure provides a workable framework within which to determine the distribution of actual tax burdens.

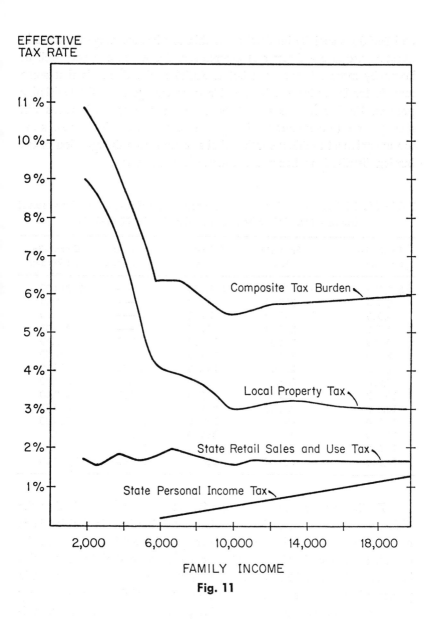

EFFECTIVE
TAX RATE

Composite Tax Burden

Local Property Tax

State Retail Sales and Use Tax

State Personal Income Tax

FAMILY INCOME

Fig. 11

allocates only 5.33 percent of its annual receipts to property, sales, *and* personal incomes taxes.

Clearly the overall pattern of burden distribution between $2,000 and $4,000 is socially intolerable. Within this income range the taxes in question produce a direct real income sacrifice which can very well be borne by more affluent households. Social equity demands that some remedy for lower-income households must emerge from the legislative process. Further increases in sales, excise, and property burdens will merely serve to compound existing injustices. The empirical results are too unequivocal to allow continued abstraction from the question of tax burden distribution when new tax measures are enacted.

Table 38. Distribution of composite property, sales-use, and personal income tax dollar burdens in California 1960–1962

Family in-come level	Property tax	Sales-use tax	Personal income tax	Composite tax burden
$ 2,000	$180.00	$ 34.00	$ ——	$ 214.00
3,000	255.00	48.60	——	303.60
4,000	288.00	74.80	——	362.80
5,000	265.00	85.00	——	350.00
6,000	246.00	108.60	8.50	363.10
7,000	273.00	140.00	18.50	431.50
8,000	296.00	149.60	28.50	474.10
9,000	306.00	162.90	38.50	507.40
10,000	310.00	175.00	48.00	533.00
12,000	384.00	204.00	82.00	670.00
14,000	434.00	233.80	118.00	785.80
16,000	480.00	265.60	156.00	901.60
18,000	540.00	295.20	210.00	1,045.20
20,000	600.00	326.00	264.00	1,190.00

Further analysis of the composite rate structure reveals that the difference in the distribution of relative tax burdens in California is narrowed significantly in the income ranges above $6,000. In fact, the overall pattern of burden distribution tends to be slightly progressive between $10,000 and $20,000. Within this range, the rate of increases in personal income tax rates is greater than the rate of decrease in property and sales tax rates. When the available evidence is weighed and considered, it appears that the pattern of burden distribution of these three taxes in income ranges above $6,000 should not be considered a matter of social concern calling for drastic legislative action or reform. Other reforms in the California state-local tax system are indicated, however.

Social policy implications

What social policy actions are suggested by the foregoing analysis? With population growing at a daily rate of 1,750 persons, it is an inescapable fact that additional tax revenues will be required to meet the future fiscal needs of the state's growing metropolitan areas.

One can see immediately that the highest social priority must attach to property tax reform in California. As the analysis of this study has revealed, property, sales and use, and various consumer excises already play a major role in the California state-local fiscal system. The existing inequities in the pattern of distribution of the burden of taxes in California reflects an historical failure to face up to the inherent limitations, administrative complexities, and the inequities of the property tax as a fiscal device in an urban-industrial society. It also reflects the failure to take a comprehensive look at the manner in which the burdens of different forms of taxation are in fact distributed over various levels of income and at the total tax burden distribution between the household and business sectors of the private economy.

State-local tax policies have tended to ignore the relevance of personal and business income as the logical base against which to correlate state and local tax burdens. The end result is a tax system which places a disproportionate burden on household units. The largest share of the real income burden of state-local taxation in California, as a consequence, falls on consumer spending. The case for reviewing the tax plight of lower-income family units already living on the edge of poverty is long overdue. Perhaps the foregoing analysis will provide a framework for significant state-local tax reform. The final chapter of this study will be devoted to a set of recommendations for tax reform and revision in the California state-local revenue system.

The fiscal future

It is one of the happy incidents of the federal system that a
single courageous state may, if its citizens choose, serve as a
laboratory, and try novel social and economic experiments
without risk to the rest of the Country.
—*Justice Louis Brandeis*

The annals of fiscal history will record that the latter half of the
decade of the 1960's was an era of significant reform in state and local
finance in California. Twenty-five years of sustained population and
economic growth, and the widely-publicized irregularities in the administration of the property tax, have forced into sharp focus the major
issues in state and local finance. Reform and revision, tempered by the
realities of the political process, are a certainty.

It goes without saying that tax revision and reform in California
should be developed within an appropriate framework of the benefit and
the ability principles of taxation. Consistent with the criteria outlined in
Chapter 4, a strong case can also be made for the implementation of an
explicitly defined set of social priorities in the program of tax reform.
These social priorities can be illustrated by one basic question: Should
highest priority be given to the promotion of the rate of economic
growth, or toward promoting greater equity in the distribution of state
and local tax burdens, or toward achieving more effective administration
of the revenue system, or toward enhancing the fiscal adequacy of state
and local tax systems? Obviously, the program of tax revision and
reform should give balanced recognition to each of these all-important
criteria.

The incredible administrative complexity associated with the local property tax must be remedied without delay; the inequitable pattern of burden distribution associated with the property tax and the conglomerate of consumption-based sales, use and excise taxes can no longer be abstracted from as new revenue sources are explored; existing urban and economic growth pressures—and the principle of complementarity between private and public goods—demand that the fiscal efficacy of the state-local revenue system be enhanced if orderly growth conditions are to be achieved.

The state of California has enjoyed uninterrupted population and economic growth since 1940. There is nothing to suggest that this rate of economic growth and development will be impeded in the near future. The basic strength of the growth forces underlying the California economy was revealed subsequent to 1960 when over 40,000 jobs in the aerospace industries were phased out by the transfer of defense and space contracts. Measured in terms of generally accepted economic indicators, the California economy continued to move ahead at a good pace. This line of analysis leads to the logical conclusion that a tax revision and reform program in California should give high priority to all of the above-mentioned criteria: effecting a more equitable pattern of distribution of tax burdens within the private sector, achieving greater administrative simplicity in the case of the property tax, and enhancing the fiscal effectiveness of the state-local tax system by correlating its revenue-generating capacities more closely with expanding personal and business incomes—the best measures of economic growth and development and ability to pay taxes. These priorities are logically determined, and socially acceptable; but they carry one basic weakness—they may not be compatible with the pressures and priorities that govern the workings of the legislative process.

Evaluation of Assembly Bill 2270—the Petris-Unruh Proposed Revenue Act of 1965

The California legislature has not been unconcerned about the growing problems of state and local finance. The Senate Fact Finding Committee on Revenue and Taxation and the Assembly Interim Committee on Revenue and Taxation were created in the 1963 session of the legislature to undertake "a comprehensive study of the tax systems presently in effect in the State of California and its local subdivisions." The Senate and Assembly committees were chaired, respectively, by Messrs. George Miller, Jr., and Nicholas C. Petris. After nearly two years of study, hearings, report preparation, and the drafting of a bill, AB 2270—the so-called Petris-Unruh bill—was introduced into the assembly on April 6, 1965. Although no action was taken on AB 2270 in the 1965 legislative session, it provides an excellent empirical reference point for analyzing and evaluating prospective revenues revision and reform programs in California.

The proposed tax legislation provided for a program of local property tax relief in an amount of $658.0 million in 1966–1967 for revenue adjustments to offset the loss in property tax revenue and to underwrite additional state expenditures. AB 2270 also incorporated a number of reforms to improve the administration of the property tax.

The property tax relief phase of AB 2270 would have narrowed the property tax base by the exemption of business inventories, household furnishings, and solvent credits. The loss in local revenues in 1966–1967 due to this provision was estimated at $287.0 million. School district property tax rates would have been reduced by an average of 25.0 percent. The estimated property tax relief under this provision would have amounted to $335.0 million in 1966–1967. This revenue loss was to be compensated for by a 1.0 percent *increase* in the state sales and use tax. Part three of the property tax reform proposal would have brought $36.0 million in special property tax relief to low-income homeowners of retirement age. Once again, the net local property tax relief was to total $358.0 million in 1966–1967.

The sponsors of AB 2270 elaborated upon the property tax relief phase of the proposed legislation in the following manner:

The reduction of the property tax base and the reduction of the school property tax rate are fully funded from tax sources other than the property tax. There will be no shifting of the property tax from one group of taxpayers to another and local government is more than completely compensated for any loss in revenue. These units will receive more revenue under the plan than they will lose. To insure that the property tax reductions are continuing, new tax ceilings will be proposed for schools and adjustments will be made for other local government entities.[1]

[1] Explanation of Revenue Act of 1965 AB 2270 (as amended May 17), (mimeo) May 25, 1965, pp. 3–4.

As we shall see shortly, AB 2270 would not have produced a shift in property tax burdens. It would, however, have produced a significant shift in state-local tax burdens *from* the business *to* the household sector. It would also have transferred over 75.0 percent of the $658.0 million property tax reduction to cigarette and retail sales taxes. These two aspects of AB 2270 will provide the focus of the analysis which follows.

The impact of AB 2270 on state and local revenues in 1966–67 was expressed in terms of a state revenue gap of $295.0 million, revenue losses due to reductions in the property tax base, $323.0 million, school district property tax relief, $335.0 million, and additional revenue for local government, $86.0 million, for a total of $1.039 billion.

The detailed estimates for each category were as follows:

	(Millions) 1966–1967
STATE REVENUE NEEDS	
Gap	$ 210
Capital improvements—pay-as-you-go	40
New program	40
State tax loss due to income tax conformity provisions	5
	$ 295
REVENUE LOSS TO GOVERNMENT DUE TO REDUCTIONS IN PROPERTY TAX BASE	
Exemption of business inventories (includes loss of state bank tax revenue of $12 million)	237
Exemption of household goods	45
Exemption of solvent credits	5
Tax relief for low-income aged	36
	$ 323
SCHOOL PROPERTY TAX RELIEF	
Mandatory school property tax reduction (average 25%)	335
	$ 335
ADDITIONAL REVENUE FOR LOCAL GOVERNMENT	
Additional assistance for cities beyond replacement of property tax loss	25
Additional assistance for counties beyond replacement of property tax loss	26
Additional assistance for schools beyond replacement for property tax loss	35
	$ 86
TOTAL	$1,039

Revenue adjustments to offset the loss of local property tax revenue and to provide for increased state needs were incorporated into AB 2270 in terms of the following specific proposals:

(1) An increase in the cigarette tax from 3 cents per pack to 8 cents per pack.

(2) A change in the income tax as follows: revising the present rate structure from 1-to-7 percent to 1-to-15 percent; reducing the personal exemption to $1,000 ($2,000 for couples); and narrowing the present tax brackets to $1,500 intervals.

(3) The adoption of a pay-as-you-earn system of collecting the state income tax, with 100 percent forgiveness from the tax (exclusive of capital gains) for 1965 income.

(4) Slight changes in the coverage of the sales tax to include the lease of equipment and the occasional sale of autos, aircraft, and boats. (Local government will also benefit from these changes under the Bradley-Burns formula.)

(5) An increase of ½ percent in the bank and corporation tax rate.

(6) A minor increase in the inheritance tax rates on inheritances over $100,000 and changes in the taxable status of capital gains at death and inheritances to tax-exempt organizations (other than churches, colleges, schools, and charitable organizations.)

(7) A property transfer tax, to be imposed by counties for their own use partially to make up for loss in property tax base. The first $15,000 of all transfers would be exempt (except for sales of bare land). The rates would be 1 percent for all transfers over $15,000 and 1½ percent for transfers over $25,000.

(8) An increase of 1 percent in the state sales tax. All the revenue from this increase will be placed in the state school fund to allow mandatory reduction of school property tax rates at an average of 25 percent.

AB 2270 called for $658.0 million in local property tax relief. How would this tax relief have been distributed between the business and household sectors? The exemption of the property tax on inventories would have provided direct relief to business of $237.0 million in 1966–1967. If we assume that 35.0 percent of the $335.0 million reduction in school district taxes accrued to the business sector, another $117.0 million of tax relief is derived. The business community would have realized a total of $354.0 million in property tax relief. When we consider that AB 2270 called for only $36.0 million in new taxes on business corporations, the Petris-Unruh bill would have provided net state-local tax relief to the business sector of $318.0 million. The obvious intent was to encourage economic growth in California. It can be questioned whether it is necessary to pay this fiscal price at a time when economic growth rates in California are highly favorable.

The specific tax reforms and revisions proposed in AB 2270 would have produced the following estimated revenue results in 1966–1967:

	(Millions) 1966–1967
Cigarette tax: 5-cent increase	$ 125
Sales tax reforms	
—taxation of equipment leases in lieu of sales	13
—taxation of occasional sales of autos, aircraft, and boats	8
Income tax	
—withholding provisions	
100 percent 1965 forgiveness (excluding capital gains)	75
—drop exemption to $1,000; narrow brackets to $1,500 intervals; extend rates to 15 percent	353
—tax capital gains at death	1
Bank and corporation tax	
—increase rate ½ percent	35
—allocation of income of multistate corporations	3
—eliminate double tax on commencing corporations	−2
Inheritance tax	
—increase rates on inheritances over $100,000	8
—tax inheritances to non-profit foundations (other than those eligible for property tax exemptions)	3 (est.)
New tax source for county use (optional)	
Property transfer tax: first $15,000 of all transactions exempt (except bare land) rates: 1 percent over $15,000; 1½ percent over $25,000	80
Automatic local revenue increase: new local sales tax revenue due to state reforms in sales tax coverage (see above)	7
1 percent sales tax increase for mandatory reduction in school property taxes and additional assistance for schools	360
New revenue sources	$1,069

AB 2270 would have in effect provided a $318.0 million tax relief bonanza to the business sector while imposing *net* new fiscal burdens in excess of $600.0 million dollars on household units in the form of higher cigarette, sales, and personal income taxes.

To be sure, the proposed revenue bill of 1965 would have improved the *pattern* of state and local tax burden distribution in California. The shift from household property taxes to the higher cigarette, sales, and personal income taxes would have reduced the overall pattern of regressivity. But, the bill would also have produced significant shifts in tax burdens from the business sector to households which already bear at least 80.0 percent of the economic incidence of state-local tax burdens in California.[2]

We can only conclude that AB 2270 would have grossly violated the system of social priorities outlined earlier in this chapter. Because of this it is fortunate that the bill was never acted upon. Future legislative proposals should place greater stress on personal and business income taxes; the wide assortment of consumer sales and excise taxes already are contributing more than a fair share of state-local revenue.

Proposals for property tax reform in California

Although students of taxation may disagree on the system of socioeconomic priorities to be implemented as new tax revenues are sought, there is unanimous agreement on the need for dramatic reform in the case of the property tax. Ideally, the property tax should be gradually phased out of the state-local revenue system of a modern urban-industrial society. Short of this, drastic reforms to improve administration, to enhance fiscal effectiveness, and to mitigate existing inequities in property taxation must be effected without delay.

It has already been suggested that significant reform in the system of taxation may evolve from an environment of fiscal crisis. Public exposure of questionable assessment practices and procedures in several California counties during 1965 gave impetus to the cry for property tax reform. AB 2270 incorporated several significant property tax reform provisions; on October 1, 1965, the California State Board of Equaliza-

---

[2] California is richly endowed with many natural resources that lend themselves to a system of severance taxation. Texas, Oklahoma, and Louisiana realize significant state revenues from a well-devised system of severance taxes. The California legislature has never seen fit to pursue with vigor this particular avenue of raising badly needed new revenues. Meanwhile, the natural resources in question are being extracted at a rapid rate.

tion made public its 15-point legislative program for constructive property taxation;[3] on November 3, 1965, the state association of county assessors of California, by resolution, adopted a 28-point legislative program "for the purpose of insuring the integrity of the property tax program . . ."[4]

Within the State Board of Equalization 15-point program, eight of the suggestions aimed to minimize, directly or indirectly, the possibility of fraudulent assessment practices; the remaining seven provisions would reduce property tax inequities. Among other things, the board asked for legislation that would make uniform assessment levels enforceable, provide reimbursements for needy citizens of retirement age, tax business inventories in proportion to their average value in the calendar year, enable law enforcement agencies to inspect now-secret property tax records, and establish a tax appeals board. One can only hope that the California legislature will give serious consideration to the board's proposed program.

Further insight into existing limitations and shortcomings of the program of property taxation in California may be gained from a review of the specific proposals contained in the state association of assessors resolution of November 3, 1965. The proposed 28-point legislative program may be summarized in these terms:

1. *Uniform Assessment Ratio:* To require each assessor and assessing agency to adopt a uniform assessment ratio within their jurisdiction, to publicly announce this ratio, and to assess all property subject to general property taxation at this announced ratio.
2. *Appeal of Ratio Findings:* In connection with the ratio findings of the State Board of Equalization, the assessor shall have recourse to the appropriate Appellate Court for the purpose of appealing the findings.
3. *Notification of Assessees:* When notification is issued under Section 619, Revenue and Taxation Code, to require the assessor to notify the assessee of the market value as well as the assessed value of his property, so the taxpayer has all information pertaining to the Assessor's value opinions and the ratio used.
4. *Assessment Appeals Board:* A proposal to change the name of the "Tax Appeals Boards" to "Assessment Appeals Boards" and to permit the

---

[3] State Board of Equalization, *Suggestions for Property Tax Legislation,* Sacramento, California, October 1, 1965.
[4] State Association of County Assessors of California, *Resolution,* Yosemite, California, November 3, 1965.

creation of such boards in any county at the discretion of their board of supervisors; to provide that assessment appeals board filing dates shall begin no sooner than upon delivery of the roll and end no later than time of issuance of tax bills; to provide qualification for the members of the Assessment Appeals Board.

5. *Inspection of Assessments Records by Public Officials:* To provide that assessor's records which are not public records and therefore not open to public inspection none-the-less shall be open to inspection by officials of authorized law enforcement agencies under specified conditions.

6. *Registration of Tax Agents:* A proposal to require tax consultants and tax agents who are retained for the purpose of representing clients in matters of property assessments to register periodically with the Division of Assessment Standards of the State Board of Equalization.

7. *Conflict of Interest—Assessors and Deputies:* To provide that no assessor shall serve as a property tax consultant or agent during a term of office or employment in an assessing capacity.

8. *Average Inventory:* To provide for the assessment of inventories for any tax year in proportion to the average value of such inventories carried during a year.

9. *Household Personal Property:* A proposal to exempt from property taxation household furnishings and personal effects used by a householder. This exemption is not to include boats, aircraft, motor vehicles, or personalty held or used in connection with a trade, profession, or business.

10. *Tax Lien Date:* A proposal to change the property tax lien date from the first Monday in March to the first day in January.

11. *Appraiser Qualifications:* A proposal to provide for qualifications examination and certification of property appraisers for taxation purposes in or on behalf of any county, for those counties who do not have Civil Service or merit exams.

12. *Reimbursement by State for Tax Exemption Losses:* A proposal providing for reimbursement by the State to local governmental jurisdictions of the loss of tax revenue resulting from state-wide exemption policies.

13. *Authority of County Assessors to Contract for Legal Services:* To provide county assessors with the authority to retain the service of attorneys in private practice for the purpose of preparing and conducting departmental litigation.

14. *Subpoena Powers of the County Board of Equalization:* To provide that the subpoena powers of a county board of equalization be expanded to require not only the attendance of witnesses, but that these witnesses may be required to bring with them any books, documents, or other things under their control.

15. *Disclosure of Information to Boards of Equalization:* A proposal provid-

ing county boards of equalization shall not make any reduction in assessed value pursuant to a petition for reduction: (1) if it is shown that the petitioner has neglected or refused to comply with any provision of law for obtaining information from taxpayers after written demand by the assessor or (2) if such person refuses to answer questions of the assessor relating to the value of the protested property.

16. *Authority to Require Information Disclosure:* A proposal to eliminate the word "personal" wherever it appears in Section 445.

17. *Application of Escaped Assessment Procedure to all Classes of Property:* To provide that escaped assessment procedures apply to all classes of property rather than just personal.

18. *Statute of Limitations Relating to Assessment of Escaped Property:* A proposal to extend the authorized time period for escape assessments to four years, instead of two years, after the lien date for the year in which the property escaped (Section 532, R & T Code).

19. *Penal Assessment:* To provide that the authorized penalties pertaining to penal assessments be fixed and not discretionary.

20. *Refund Claim Filing Period:* To provide that the filing period for tax refund claims be set at one year, rather than three years, after making the payment sought to be refunded.

21. *Six-months Summons Procedure in Tax Recovery Actions:* To provide that, in an action either to recover taxes paid under protest or to recover taxes upon which a claim for refund has been rejected by the board of supervisors, the summons procedure must be initiated and completed within six months after the commencement of the action.

22. *Assessee's Error as a Basis for Tax Refund:* A proposal to establish as a basis for tax refund, excessive or improper assessments directly attributable to erroneous property information supplied by the assessee.

23. *Total Property Value as a Basis for Equalizing Assessments:* To provide that equalizing bodies in their determination of an equitable assessment be governed by the relationship of the total assessment to the total market value of the property, specifically, that no reduction in assessed valuation shall be granted unless the total property value so indicates.

24. *Provision for Separate Assessment of Land and Improvements only when there is a Separate Tax on Land:* To provide that land, and the improvements thereon, be separately assessed only in those revenue districts in which there is a separate tax levied on land alone.

25. *Consigned and Leased Property:* To provide that personal property on consignment or on lease, shall be assessed either to the consignee or to the consignor, or to the lessee or to the lessor, or to both.

26. *Provision for Taxation of Possessory Interests:* To provide that possessory interests in personal property and real property shall be subject to taxation to the same extent as though the possessor were the owner.

6. The fiscal future

27. *Property Tax Relief for Senior Citizens:* A proposal to institute a program of property tax relief for California resident low income senior citizens by means of a state administered grant system providing for scheduled reimbursement of property taxes, both direct and indirect.
28. *Veteran Exemption Qualification:* A proposal requesting the enactment of legislation which will clarify and make consistent the standard applied to the property value qualification for veterans' exemption by requiring that the standard of value of all assets including real and personal property be 100% of market value.

The property tax reform measures incorporated in AB 2270, along with those proposed by the State Board of Equalization and the county assessors, provide a convenient focus for a future legislative program. If the property tax is to remain as an integral part of California's state-local revenue system, two basic types of reform and/or revision are called for. First, the administration of the tax must be improved considerably, particularly in the matter of the valuations assigned to different types of property. Genuine intercounty equalization is an absolute must; properties currently being favored in the assessment process must be brought back into line. Second, existing inequities in the distribution of property tax burdens must be reduced. The existing "system" of exemptions demands a rational review. For example, what is the social rationale for the exemption of financial claims to wealth, e.g., stocks, bonds, mortgages, deeds of trust, from the property tax base? We have already documented the steep pattern of regressivity that governs the distribution of property tax burdens over different ranges of household income.

The federal tax-turnback proposal

The federal tax-turnback proposal has been under discussion in fiscal circles for the past decade. Under this program the federal government would share a given percentage of income tax revenues with the 50 states. The effect would be that of shifting a portion of the growing state-local revenue burden from regressive sales and property taxes to the progressive federal income tax.

During 1964 there were indications that a program of federal tax turnbacks to the states might be initiated. The program, however, found its temporary demise in the inner workings of the political process.

Should proper reform in the state-local fiscal system in the United States not be forthcoming within the next several years, a strong case could be made for use of the tax turnback device. In many respects this would simply involve an extension of the federal grant programs already well institutionalized on the expenditure side. There are a number of issues relating to the program currently under discussion.[5] However, chances for initiating the federal tax turnback program in the near term have lessened as costs of national defense have increased. In fact, near the end of 1965, there was serious speculation concerning increases in federal tax rates to meet the new expenditure requirements of both defense and the social legislation of the early 1960's. In retrospect, the $11.0 billion federal tax reduction program of 1964 appears to have been ill-timed, ill-conceived, and conducive to additional budgetary deficits and inflation.

The state-local shared income tax

Having reviewed the facts, the problems, and the policy implications of state and local finance in California, this section will present a positive program of taxation—one geared to meet the fiscal needs of the future. This program is governed by the economic realities of the urban-industrial society which typifies the California of the 1960's. The proposals, moreover, are conditioned by the simple fact that most, if not all, taxes in modern society are paid out of income—the wages and salaries, the rents, interests, and the profits that accrue to economic units in the private sector. Why not, then, correlate tax burdens directly with income, and avoid the use of outmoded taxes that promote inequities, fiscal inadequacy, administrative complexity, and economic inefficiencies?[6]

The real key to state and local taxation in California rests with the

---

[5] For an excellent recent discussion of these issues, see "Sharing Federal Revenues With the States" by C. Lowell Harriss, *The New Economics: Implications for Business,* (Tax Foundation, Inc., New York, 1966), pp. 53–61.

[6] This suggests that the property tax be gradually phased out of the local revenue structure and that new sources be made available to local units of government.

introduction of a state-local shared income tax into the revenue system. Under the proposed California state-local shared income tax, a local income tax would become an integral part of the existing state income tax system. Local units of government—cities, counties, and school districts—would be given the authority to levy a personal *and* business income tax. The local personal income tax rate structure would allow for a moderate degree of progressivity. The tax base would be the generally accepted measure of business and personal taxable income used at the state level. In every sense, both the local personal and business income tax would be integrated into the existing system of state income taxation.

It is important to stress that the proposed state-local shared income tax does not envision piecemeal income tax legislation of the type which created the payroll taxes found in certain American cities. On the contrary, legislation would be general and would bring income tax revenues to all units of local government with the exception of special districts. This would in effect break down the existing "islands" of income.

The broad outline of a state-local shared income tax program in California can be described in these terms: First, existing state personal and corporation and bank income tax rates would be increased moderately to provide new tax revenues for local government; second, the personal and business income tax bases currently used for state tax purposes would be used for local purposes; third, state personal and business income tax returns would be revised to provide space for the calculation and reflection of local income tax liabilities; fourth, local income taxes would be paid to the State Franchise Tax Board or other collection agency, as appropriate; fifth, the local income tax proceeds would be shared with counties, cities, and school districts under a set of formulas reflecting such factors as population, number of households, school enrollments, per capita assessed valuations, etc. There undoubtedly will be the problem of developing a set of formulas satisfactory to the local jurisdictions concerned. The problem, however, can be met.

Is the state-local shared income tax a revolutionary fiscal proposal? Not really. It involves the creation of no new tax agencies; it avoids the cumbersome problem of direct administration at the local level; no new tax procedural responsibilities are placed upon individuals and businesses as the proposal is built upon tax procedures and programs already in effect at the state level.[7]

The most important feature of the state-local shared income tax is that the local revenue system would be tied closely to the growing level of income which represents the best measure of economic growth and progress in the local and state economies. Also important, the proposal would correlate the distribution of tax burdens more closely with the ability-to-pay principle of taxation. This would indeed be a revolutionary development in local public finance. From the social value point of view, this would mitigate the great inequities associated with the manner in which existing property tax burdens are distributed. Introduction of the income tax at the local level of government would also enhance the degree of local autonomy in government. Finally, greater balance in the state-local revenue system would be achieved. Unless the revenue system of local government is strengthened by property tax reform and the introduction of new primary sources of tax revenue, the fiscal dominance of higher levels of government will continue to expand as the pressures of urbanization increase.

[7] Retail sales and use and motor vehicle revenues are collected by state tax agencies and returned to local units of government.

Index

Taxation (continued)
  and expenditure, concept of fiscal
      equity, 59
  local, 13–33
  progressivity concept, 58
  proportionality concept, 58
  reforms needed, 61, 86–99
  regressivity in, 26, 59, 76, 77,
      79, 82
  state, 34–54
  state-local:
    implication of urbanization, 9

Taxation (continued)
    policy framework for, 55–61

U

Urbanization, 1–12, 63
  development of urban complexes,
      10
  fiscal implications of, 9
  low-density land use pattern, 10